THE BRAIN

Magnificent Mind Machine

ALSO BY MARGERY AND HOWARD FACKLAM
From Cell to Clone:
  The Story of Genetic Engineering

ALSO BY MARGERY FACKLAM
Frozen Snakes and Dinosaur Bones:
  Exploring a Natural History Museum

Wild Animals, Gentle Women

MARGERY AND
HOWARD FACKLAM

ILLUSTRATED WITH DRAWINGS
BY PAUL FACKLAM
AND WITH PHOTOGRAPHS

Magnificent Mind

THE BRAIN

Machine

HARCOURT BRACE JOVANOVICH, PUBLISHERS
NEW YORK AND LONDON

For Jeffery David Facklam

Requests for permission to make copies of
any part of the work should be mailed to:
Permissions, Harcourt Brace Jovanovich, Publishers,
757 Third Avenue, New York, New York 10017.

Printed in the United States of America

LIBRARY OF CONGRESS CATALOGING IN PUBLICATION DATA
Facklam, Margery.
The brain.
Bibliography: p.   Includes index.
1. Brain.   I. Facklam, Howard.   II. Title.
QP376.F27   612′.82   81–47529
ISBN 0–15–211388–6   AACR2

B C D E   First edition

Contents

THE BRAIN

Magnificent Mind Machine

In this book, wherever the word man *appears, unless referring to a specific person, it means humankind, a species of animal that includes both male and female. The use of* he/she, him/her, *or* his/hers *is distracting for the reader, so we use* he, him, *and* his *throughout.*

1 *The Ghost in the Machine*

Dr. Prentice adjusted the clamp that regulated the flow of nutrient solution into the round glass tank. He checked the oxygen that fed into the blood dripping into a tube embedded in the mass of pink-gray tissue awash in the clear liquid. He bent closer. No matter how often he watched this human brain, he found it breathtaking.

Motionless, silent, but somehow alive, it looked like an enormous unshelled walnut. Dozens of wires as fine as spider silk jutted from the brain, some embedded deeply, others just below the lumpy surface. Each wire led from an electrode implanted in the brain to one of the terminals in the computers that lined the laboratory.

Although looking at this bodyless brain sometimes gave him a moment of unease, Prentice did not feel guilty about the experiment. The body that once housed this brain had been crushed beyond recognition in an automobile accident. The medical information on the body's ID bracelet indicated that all organs were to be donated to science at death, and after all, Prentice told himself, the brain was just another organ.

Decades before Prentice had even thought of medicine as a career, biological death had been set by law as that moment when brain waves no longer registered on an EEG machine. After the accident, this brain had still registered vague, irregular waves, but since the lungs, kidneys, and heart had been destroyed beyond repair or the possibility of use for transplant, the family had signed permission papers for the brain to be used.

During the first month of the experiment, Dr. Prentice had worked only to nourish this brain, to keep it alive. He did not expect more. But as weeks went by and the brain wave pattern became stronger, Prentice began to hope that the code of the electrochemical impulses produced by the brain might translate into letters and maybe words he had programed into the computer.

Now Prentice stood up, stretched, and walked to the computers. The printout key was on. The paper rolled silently off the cylinder, the needle riding the slow waves, recording the slightest brain activity.

He watched for several seconds. Prentice had a strong urge to stay, but he had promised his wife to be home early for once. Absently he patted the computer's gray steel side. He zipped his jacket, picked up his Thermos and a stack of papers, and switched off the lights. He turned to glance at the tank once more. Moonlight streamed through the window, shimmering on the thick fluid, sparkling from the wires in the brain. It seemed to Dr. Prentice that tonight the brain looked so alive it almost glowed with vitality. A shiver ran down his spine. It must be getting colder, he thought, and he turned up his jacket collar.

As he reached for the doorknob, the clatter of the computer printout went through him like machine-gun fire in the silent room. Prentice whirled, dropping his papers. The Thermos crashed to the floor. He groped for the light switch. It seemed ages before he could see.

He leaned over the keyboard, trembling. Only one or two letters had ever appeared before, and those, he was certain, had been accidents, some loose connection, some short circuit from the ten volts of electricity that ran the human brain.

This was more than a smattering of accidental letters. His eyes widened. "My God," he gasped.

"S-T-A-Y," the computer printed, repeating with no hesitation, "Stay. Do not leave me."

Of course this is science fiction, fiction designed to make the reader's skin crawl, to send shivers down the spine. No such message—no message of any kind—has come from a human brain without a body, but some of brain research today sounds like science fiction. It raises the hair on the back of the neck, goose bumps on the arms, to know that at the flip of a switch a cat stalking a mouse can suddenly become frightened to death of the mouse, can turn from hunter to hunted.

Connect the proper wire, and a docile monkey becomes a vicious attacker. Press a button, and a charging bull stops dead in its tracks. Insert a needle into the front of a man's brain, and his personality changes. Implant an electrode in a person's brain and monitor his thoughts, and it is possible to know when the subject so much as thinks "yes" or "no." Inject a chemical, and a person can learn more quickly or forget completely. Probe another spot, and an event from the past can be replayed as though it were just happening.

Carl Sagan, Pulitzer Prize–winning scientist and writer, has suggested that brain research goes against some deep instincts that have served mankind well, dredging up fears born in our primitive past. Brain experiments go against some feelings long hidden for the sake of survival, built into our genes to keep us alive.

Primitive tribes hung skulls on trees to warn trespassers to stay out or lose their heads. The symbol of skull and crossbones still serves as a warning of danger or death. We use it on poisons to warn, "Keep out or lose your life." There is, after all, a great advantage to those who avoid losing their heads, who run to live another day, to pass on those same survival instincts and skills to the next generation. Evolution favored the ever more intelligent brain.

But Sagan has also suggested that it is time to put down such "emotional baggage" and get on with breaking the code of the brain, the last great frontier of science.

In the 1940s human brains unlocked the secret of the atomic code, and we had to learn—are still learning—how to cope with both good and evil uses of the powerful atom. In the 1960s human brains broke the genetic code when they learned how DNA carries the patterns of our inheritance. From that code scientists have learned to combine genes, to repair them, and to change them. Even though there are those who predict more evil than good from such powerful knowledge, it is to be hoped that the information will be advantageous for mankind.

All investigations carry with them some element of risk. There is no money-back guarantee that anything in nature will live up to our ideas. Man needs to learn about his own brain for his own survival.

Like every branch of science, the study of the brain has progressed step by daily step with a now and then Eureka! discovery along the way to boost it to a new level of understanding. But brain research has been slower than most sciences, not only because it had to wait for more sophisticated equipment, but also because the brain is more than just a piece of machinery, more than just another part of the body. It is the operational center of that elusive thing called the mind. Even now, the brain is referred to by many scientists as the ghost in the machine.

A heart is a heart. A heart can be transplanted from one person to another. A heart can be repaired, new valves put in, new arteries built, and the heartbeat regulated by an electronic pacemaker implanted under the skin. A body can lose arms, legs, eyes, a lung, a kidney, parts of the stomach and intestines, the entire reproductive system, and the patient remains the same person.

Not so the brain. More than one scientist has wondered, "If you transplant a brain, whose home does the patient return to?" Is it a brain transplant or a body transplant?

It seems so obvious in this decade that who we are and what we are is centered in those three pounds (6½ kilograms) of tissue, in the 100 billion cells of the brain, that it is difficult to imagine how anyone could have doubted that. It is astonishing that it would not be obvious because of the way the brain is protected, totally surrounded by a hard casing of bone.

We tend to believe what we see. At one time people believed that the brain was a concentration of mucus that leaked out during the common cold. Anyone with a cold can understand how that story started.

Not only do we believe what we see, but also what we feel,

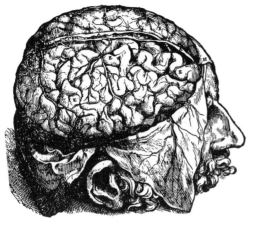

*An early engraving showing
a dissection of the brain
by anatomist Vesalius.*
(BAKKEN MUSEUM OF ELECTRICITY IN LIFE)

and except for occasional headaches, who can feel the brain at work? We do feel the heart, feel it pounding when we're scared, feel it "in our throat" when we are anxious and upset. The heart feels alive. It circulates the blood, and when too much blood leaks out, life goes, too. It is easy to see how the connection was made between the heart and the soul or spirit. If a soul or spirit departs at death, it must reside somewhere in the body during life. For most of history, man has given that place to the heart.

We have daily reminders of that ancient idea, phrases we say and sing without thinking: I love you with all my heart. My heart's desire. I know in my heart. His heart was broken. Her heart rules her head. But it is the brain that allows us to love or hate, create or destroy, laugh or cry.

In ancient Egypt the heart was removed from the corpse, mummified separately, and buried in an urn or returned to the mummy so that it could accompany the owner to his new life, where it would be weighed for its goodness. The brain, however, had little use in the afterlife, judging by the custom of removing it before burial. Jürgen Thorwald described the process: "They take first a crooked piece of iron, and with it draw out the brain through the nostrils, thus getting rid of a portion, while the skull is cleared of the rest by rinsing with drugs." So much for the brain.

The brain has been compared to a telephone switchboard with its incoming and outgoing calls, to a tape recorder able to record and play back, to a computer that can decipher, organize information, and answer problems. The brain is at once none of these and all of these. It is more complex than anything devised by man and the most intricate object of nature as well.

A computer large enough to handle information processed by the average brain would not fit into the Empire State Building and would require the entire energy output of Niagara Falls, with the Niagara River to cool it. Even if such a computer-brain could be built, it would not know compassion, joy, or grief.

How do we know what we know? How do we think? How do we learn? How do we remember?

Until recently, the brain has been studied from the outside, known only by its reactions, by what it does. Today it is studied at many levels, from the molecules at each synapse to the behavior of an entire species.

And yet, Francis Crick, who shared the Nobel Prize with James Watson and Maurice Wilkins for the discovery of the structure of the DNA molecule, has pointed out that "in spite of the steady accumulation of detailed knowledge, how the human brain works is still profoundly mysterious."

Imagine—and we think imagination is unique to the human brain—the information processed by the ten billion neurons for a simple activity like playing basketball in the yard with a few friends. Without your really thinking about it, you coordinate your muscles so that they move feet and arms. You keep your eye on the ball, on the hoop, and on other players. You make a long hook shot, and the ball falls neatly through the hoop. You smile and feel a surge of confidence, of well-being, and you don't think about all the muscles that make the smile. In your mind's eye you see yourself as a pro.

You see the dog leap off the porch and dart between two of the players as he chases the ball. You manage to avoid tripping over the dog as you yell at him. You hear the radio playing in the house and recognize the music, which makes you think of a dance next week and wonder whom you'll go with. A mosquito lands on your arm, stings, and absently you swat at it. Reacting to the heat, you sweat and wipe your forehead without much thought. You squint in the sunlight and perhaps remember where you left your sunglasses.

The phone rings. You hear it and wonder if it's for you. And during all these fleeting thoughts and reactions, you are talking with your friends, hearing their words, sorting and storing information. One day in the future you will remember this game and joke about the dog trying to get the ball. You smell cookies baking, and suddenly you are aware of hunger. You keep breathing, your heart beats steadily, and all systems work together, every one of them coordinated by the brain.

How does it all work?

Millions of dollars are spent on brain research each year in the United States alone, and more millions around the world. Entire laboratories are devoted to learning how brain chemicals work, or how people sleep, or how drugs alter the mind. While some researchers are looking for answers to the basic biological and chemical questions, others are looking for ways to retard the aging process, ways to eliminate pain with nonaddictive drugs or by using the brain's own pain-blocking drugs. Some look for ways to cure mental disorders such as schizophrenia, ways to allow the blind to see and the deaf to hear through devices implanted in the brain. Some study ways to eliminate violence or make learning easier. The search is on for ways to prevent strokes, to eliminate tumors, to repair brains damaged by disease or accident, to expand creativity, and to increase intelligence.

There are those who believe that eventually it will be possible to know the how and why of every thought, to know the brain as a great mind machine, as knowable as the engine of a car. But others echo the feelings of Nobel Prize–winning brain scientist Sir John Eccles, who said in a recent interview, "I go all the way with my fellow scientists in understanding the brain physically. But it doesn't explain me, or human choice, delight, courage, or compassion. I think we must go beyond. So I'm a heretic, a dualist who firmly believes that there is something apart from all the electricity and chemistry we can measure. I think there is more wonder and mystery than we realize."

And that has been the ghost in the machine, the question that has made brain research different from any other. The mind and the brain, are they the same? Will the human brain ever be able to analyze its own mind, or will the human mind ever be able to analyze its own brain?

2 *Is Bigger Better?*

The human brain is like a rambling old house that has been enlarged and changed to accommodate the needs of a growing family. The house began as a one-room cottage, but a porch was added, a wing put on, a room enlarged and remodeled. New systems were put in, pipes and faucets replacing the simpler systems of chamber pots and hand pumps. A room that once served only as shelter now houses a color television, a telephone, an intercom, a tape recorder, and a computer.

Like the old house, man's brain is built room upon room on top of a foundation of ganglia, a mass of neurons that still serves the lowly earthworm. Through millions of years, that lump of nerve cells developed and expanded. It added more complex systems to accommodate the needs of animals that ventured farther into the environment, emerged from water to land to air, changed from hunted to hunter. Each change required better senses of sight or touch or smell. With each adaptation for survival, whether it was increased speed or better communication, the brain changed.

Understanding how the brain works begins with the first rooms of the old brain-house. The most primitive vertebrates have brains that look like three irregular swellings at the front of the

An early diagram showing the functions of the brain

Is Bigger Better? 9

spinal cord. In more complex animals, the fishes, amphibians, reptiles, and mammals, these three swellings specialized and changed in size and shape. Parts of the brain developed in different animals to handle the activities those animals needed in order to survive.

The first swelling of the spinal cord, the hindbrain, or brain stem, was and still is for self-preservation. The medulla oblongata, only a thickening of the spinal cord in fishes, still regulates our life-support systems—the circulating of the blood, the beat of the heart, swallowing, and breathing.

The bump on top of the hindbrain is an outgrowth of the medulla called the cerebellum, the "little brain." It is the two-layered cerebellum that coordinates balance, movement, and posture. It is the cerebellum that puts muscles into automatic sequence when it gets such messages as "Pick up the Frisbee" or "Scratch your head." The cerebellum allows us to shift into automatic when we play the piano or hit a tennis ball after long practice. Practice trains the cerebellum. If any portion of the brain can be decoded entirely, scientists believe it will be the computerlike cerebellum.

The old midbrain that was such an important part of the control center of early vertebrates has decreased in man, overshadowed by the great forebrain. What little there is left of the midbrain has combined with the hindbrain into an area some scientists call the R complex, or the reptilian complex. Giving us a sense of territory, the old reptilian brain still dictates many of our actions involved in age-old rituals that we can't seem to escape. One researcher describes the route he walks to work each morning as unchanging and automatic, dictated by his old reptilian brain.

The forebrain is the part of the ancient brain that has changed the most. It is generally divided into two major sections; the front of the old forebrain became the all-important cerebrum, and the remainder consists of a group of structures that together are known as the limbic system. It is a caplike ring of tissue on top of the old brain stem made up of the thalamus, hypothalamus, amygdala, pituitary gland, and the hippocampus.

The thalamus is part of an area of the brain known as the arousal system. It is a wiretapping center, a place where incoming and outgoing messages from all parts of the brain are monitored and are either sent through for action or stopped. We are continu-

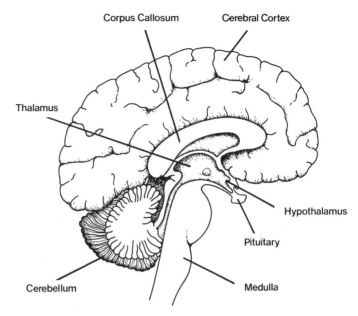

Corpus Callosum   Cerebral Cortex

Thalamus

Hypothalamus

Pituitary

Cerebellum   Medulla

Cross section showing parts of the human brain

ously getting stimulation from every direction, both inside and outside the body, chemical messages from taste and smell, mechanical messages from touch, messages of sight and sound. If we reacted to each of these, we would become totally disorganized. The thalamus filters out messages, and it also sends messages to the spinal cord to block some information even before it gets to the brain. If you are intently watching television or are absorbed in reading a book, you may not hear your mother call or feel her touch on your shoulder. When you put on clothes, at first you feel the smoothness of the shirt, the rougher texture of the jacket, the fit of the sneakers. But these senses are filtered out during the day, unless one sensation becomes greatly increased. If your shoes pinch, the bombardment of that message will get through the filter system.

Just below the thalamus is the hypothalamus, the controller of emotions, the place of pain or pleasure, rage or calm. This is the part of the limbic system that controls hunger, thirst, body temperature, blood pressure, sexual feelings.

The cerebrum is the room at the top, the part of the old house that makes man the most intelligent animal. The ancient cerebrum, like that of fishes today, was little more than a relay center for the sense of smell, the location of the olfactory lobes. In amphibians who came onto land and needed to respond to more complicated information, the cerebrum expanded into a surface layer called the cortex (meaning outer rind or bark), but it was still only a sight-and-smell machine that allowed the animals to find food and avoid enemies.

In reptiles this cortex developed further as they learned to live more completely on land, no longer laying eggs in the protection of water but finding places on land that would be safe. Early mammals grew an even larger layer called the neocortex.

It is this neocortex that grew and grew until it had to fold and crumple to fit into the skull. Like a magician's scarf folding into a hollow egg, the changing brain folded into convolutions, providing a greater surface area for brain cells to process information.

A simple brain may offer one response to a stimulus. A frog sees the movement and pattern that tells its brain to flick out the sticky tongue in response, and the frog will flick the tongue whether the food is real or not.

Areas of brain function

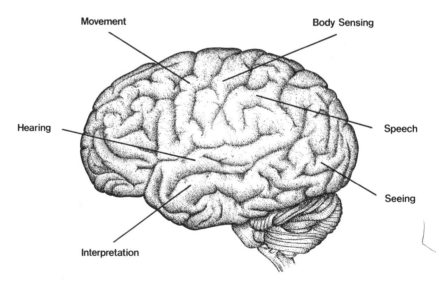

Movement   Body Sensing

Hearing   Speech

Seeing

Interpretation

Larger brains have room for a greater number and variety of responses. A fox can see and smell and hear a mouse. It processes that information and will respond, by pouncing, or by waiting for a better chance, or by ignoring the prey.

As animals developed, their brains became more complex and larger, but the size of the animal has little to do with intelligence. The mighty dinosaurs are proof of that. The stegosaurus weighed more than 10 tons (9.09 metric tons), twice the weight of a big elephant, but it was a stupid animal. Its brain was about as big as a cat's. In order to move its enormous hind legs and clumsy tail, it developed a second brain, a collection of nerve cells at the base of the spine. This spinal brain let the beast know when it had stepped into a hot spring or caught its foot between rocks. Dinosaurs were successful animals for millions of years, dominating the earth. They became extinct for a variety of reasons, not least of which was that their small brains did not allow them to adapt to changes in their environment.

The mammal brain, on the other hand, grew richer as its cerebral cortex, this new roof-brain, allowed it to handle more complicated information. But size did not determine intelligence. A large cow is not as bright as a small dog. The brains of whales and elephants are not only enormous, but also greatly convoluted. But they need such a large part of the brain just to coordinate their huge bodies that there isn't much left over for other functions.

There are those who claim whales and dolphins are as smart as or smarter than man because their brains are more convoluted. There are no maps of whale brains, and it is almost impossible to carry out brain studies on such rare, elusive animals.

John Lilly gave up his research on dolphins and their language when he began to feel that he was intruding on the lives of intelligent beings, that he was imprisoning them. Other biologists strongly disagree with Lilly. Several facts remain unchallenged, however. One on which all agree is that whales and dolphins cannot be compared to primates or man because they do not have hands. Our hands, manipulating things, making tools, allow us to live as we do. Our intelligence is based on our handedness. Whales and dolphins live in an entirely different world, an environment of water in which they are superior because they have developed a complex communication system we do not now and may never understand. In *Mind in the Waters,* Joan McIntyre, a scientist who

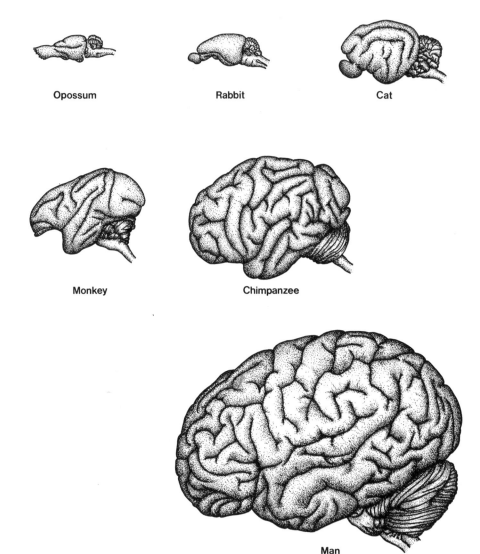

Comparative brain sizes

studies whales and dolphins, wrote, "We must continue to be haunted by such solitary beings with amazingly complex brains wending their way through the seas, wondering, perhaps, what manner of men are hunting them down to destroy them forever."

Man's brain, with its highly convoluted, thick cortex rich in nerve connections, is the largest brain in comparison to body size.

That is the key: size of body compared to size of brain, as well as the number of convolutions and the thickness of the cortex. Man's roof-brain takes up five-sixths of the mass of his whole brain. It is the thinking cap built upon the ancient brain, growing over and around the other parts. The cerebrum has two halves, called the right and left hemispheres, which look like two halves of an unshelled walnut.

A newborn baby's brain weighs about twelve ounces, or 350 grams, and the average adult brain weighs about three pounds, or 1,375 grams. The infant brain has all the nerve cells it will ever have. The change in size comes through learning and experience, building richer and larger connections.

Within a species brain size means nothing. A genius may have a brain smaller than a mentally retarded person's. Criminals' brains are on the average not different in size from priests' and school principals'. Einstein's brain was not unusually large. A woman's brain is about nine cubic inches, or 150 cubic centimeters, smaller than man's, but her body size is proportionately smaller as well. Brain size differs among groups of people. Orientals generally have slightly larger brains than whites, but in controlled tests the two groups are similar.

During the first three years of life, the time of most rapid learning, the brain grows fastest. By the time a child is six, the brain has grown to 90 percent of its adult size. There are about 100 billion cells in the brain. Some ten billion of them are neurons, the electrochemical switches that send the messages. As learning takes place, the number of the cells remains the same, but the number of connections of each cell increases. Cells damaged from drugs, alcohol, aging, disease, or accident are never replaced.

These neurons are not nicely regular cells, neither round, like red blood cells, nor neat brick shapes or honeycombs. Neurons look like strung-out petunias with a stem that can stretch from the brain to the base of the spine. This irregular cell body consists of all the necessary parts, of cytoplasm and nucleus, but it straggles off into countless fine branches called dendrites. These dendrites bring messages to the cell. Messages are carried away from the cell by the long stem called the axon.

Each neuron is a self-contained power unit, the source of its own energy supply. It is either on or off, either firing or not firing across the gap between the axon of one cell and the dendrite of another. This gap is called the synapse. No one has ever counted the synapses in the brain, but a guess of 100 trillion connections is certainly reasonable. All of these connections are organized into tightly woven circuits.

Three kinds of neurons are in constant action. The sensors detect environmental changes inside or outside the body. The interneurons process that information. The motoneurons activate the muscles to respond.

The other ninety billion cells are called the glial, or glue, cells. At first they were considered unimportant, merely glue to hold the rest of the brain together. But recent research is assigning other functions to them, calling them the housekeepers, the nourishing cells. They may be part of the important blood-brain barrier that keeps viruses and bacteria and other undesirable material from getting into the brain. Most recent, and most interesting, are findings that suggest the glial cells are part of the incredible memory-storage system.

Encased in the hard skull, the brain is well protected from outside forces. Inside it is further protected by three layers of tissue called the meninges. The layer over the brain is the pia mater. The layer lining the skull is the dura mater, and sandwiched in between is the arachnoid. Further protecting and cushioning the brain and spinal cord is the cerebrospinal fluid that continuously washes through hollow compartments called ventricles.

The brain can feel no pain. It can be poked, probed with electric currents, or cut, and its owner feels nothing. Once the skull is opened under anesthetic, the living brain can be examined and can have things implanted in it that will never be felt.

Mapping the brain is not much further along than mapping the world was when Columbus set out on his big trip. But we are far ahead of the Greek philosopher Aristotle, who talked about the brain as a cooling place for circulating blood. We are also far ahead of a discouraged scientist who wrote in 1846, "The anatomy of the intimate structures of the brain is and remains apparently a book sealed with seven seals and written moreover in hieroglyphics."

The seals have been broken, and some of the hieroglyphics have been deciphered.

3 *Electric Frogs*

The science of neurology began in earnest with frog legs in a butcher shop in Bologna, Italy, or so it seems from stories about Luigi Galvani, the father of modern neurology.

Galvani, an anatomy professor at the University of Bologna, walked by a butcher shop one stormy evening and saw freshly killed frogs hanging on hooks. He noticed that the frogs' muscles twitched and jumped when they touched the metal base of the hooks.

It was 1771, and the science of the decade was electricity. The Leyden jar had been invented. A metal-lined glass jar with a rod sticking out of a cork, it was used to store static electricity. If you touch a Leyden jar, you get a shock, and if you put a metal strip near the rod, a spark jumps across the gap. In the 1750s papers had been published describing how muscles of dead animals contract when touched by the Leyden jar.

Galvani tested the theory that electricity from the atmosphere could cause animals' muscles to move as they did when touched by the Leyden jar. He had put a wire over his roof and down into the laboratory. During an electrical storm he touched the wire to frogs' legs, and their muscles did twitch. He was as lucky as Ben Franklin had been when he flew his kite in the storm. Both men took an enormous chance of being burned to a crisp by lightning.

When Galvani saw the frogs in the butcher shop, he began to think the electricity might come from the metal hooks rather than from the atmosphere. He bought a batch of frogs, put them on hooks, and hung them on the iron railing of his porch. If he happened to push the frog against the railing as he hung it up, the frog's legs jerked. He set up further experiments that then led him to believe the electricity was generated in the animal itself and only discharged when it touched the two metals.

Animal electricity was not a new idea. People had seen electric eels and torpedo fish, more commonly called tremble fish. Early Greek records told of doctors who treated high fevers by touching patients with the tremble fish. Patients suffering from gout were made to stand on an electric fish. No one knew how this

A 1791 engraving showing Galvani's laboratory set up for his experiments on frog legs (BAKKEN MUSEUM OF ELECTRICITY IN LIFE)

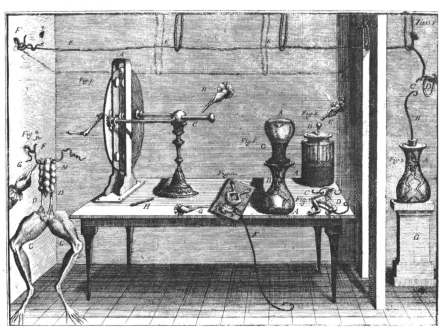

worked, only that the fish had power that would "enter into his hands who toucheth it."

When Galvani completed his experiment, he sent the results to his friend Alessandro Volta. Volta was a physicist, a fact that may have surprised his family. They had thought him retarded because he did not talk until he was four years old. (It may have been lack of opportunity; he was one of nine children.) He made up for lost time, however, and by the age of fourteen, he had decided on a career in physics.

Reading Galvani's papers, Volta at first agreed with the idea of animal electricity. Later he changed his mind, preferring to stay with the idea—which proved to be the right one—that the contact of two different metals produced the electricity that stimulated the muscle contraction.

Both men published their ideas, and the debate raged for years. Volta went on to other discoveries and became famous when he invented the first battery. His name was given to the unit of force that moves electricity, the volt.

Galvani, who was an extremely shy man, became discouraged but continued to believe in and study animal electricity. After his death his name was given to the kind of electricity set up by two metals in contact, galvanic electricity. Although his experiments did not prove what he thought they did, his work did start serious investigation into the electrical nature of the nerve impulse. Galvani thought of the brain as the source of an animal's electricity, which travels through the nerves to the muscles. He thought of the muscle fibers as tiny Leyden jars, condensing and storing electricity, discharging it when in contact with metal. Galvani was headed in the right direction.

The public controversy between Volta and Galvani provoked interest in the question. Other scientists turned to solving the age-old problem of how the nervous system sends its messages.

For 1,500 years science clung to the theory of a Greek physician for this explanation. When Claudius Galenus (Galen) finished medical college about 159 A.D., he was assigned to the gladiator training school. There he had ample opportunity to study anatomy as he patched up injured fighters. One of his patients was the gladiator Pausania, who had been thrown from a chariot, injuring his spine. One of the gladiator's hands was numb, although he could move his fingers.

Galen had always thought there were two pathways for the nerves, one for the senses (sensory) and the other for physical activity (motor). This patient seemed to prove that theory. Although Pausania's sensory pathway to the hand was blocked, his motor pathway was all right.

The Greek doctor followed up with a series of experiments in which he cut different sections of animals' spinal cords to see what pathways had been destroyed. Unfortunately, there were no anesthetics as there are today for experimental animals.

Next Galen tried to explain what traveled along these pathways of the nervous system. He decided the tubes must be hollow and that a substance he called animal spirits circulated from the hollow ventricles in the brain to all parts of the body. He believed food digested in the stomach went into the liver, where it turned into "natural spirits," which then went to the right side of the heart. In the heart they changed to "vital spirits," which were pumped to the brain, where they became "animal spirits."

Galen's idea of animal spirits remained the accepted one. No one proposed anything better, and it fit with the teachings of the church. As late as 1671, a doctor in London described cases in which accident or disease had prevented blood from getting to patients' brains. As a result, nerve function stopped because the vital spirits could not get to the ventricles of the brain where they would be turned into animal spirits.

Then Galvani's suggestion of animal electricity, inaccurate as it was, became the idea that would not go away. In fact, a few decades after Galvani's time, Mary Wollstonecraft Shelley, wife of the poet, wrote the amazing science-fiction tale about Dr. Frankenstein's monster who came to life through a jolt of electricity.

But many years went by before more could be added to the puzzle of how the nerves really worked. Technology had to catch up. The usual way of detecting electricity was by feeling a shock (causing muscles to twitch) or seeing a spark. There were no instruments to measure it. Then in 1820 just such a piece of equipment was made, and in honor of Galvani it was called the galvanometer. It measured the strength of electricity going through a coil of wire, making a magnetized needle move, but it was not sensitive enough to pick up the tiny currents in living cells.

Twenty years went by. Emil Du Bois-Reymond was a graduate student at the University of Berlin in 1843, when he wrote a paper on electric fishes. His professor, Johannes Müller, had an international reputation for his own biological discoveries as well as for training students who became famous. When he finished graduate school, Du Bois-Reymond continued his interest in electricity in animal tissue, but he had no way to measure it. Finally he made his own galvanometer of the purest, finest copper wire he could find. The purity assured him there would be no tiny particles of iron to affect the magnetic needle, and the fineness of wire allowed him to make many coils and still keep the instrument lightweight as well as sensitive.

He put the wires on a nerve in a frog's leg. Nothing happened. Then he hit upon the idea of making a tiny cut in a nerve. When he put one wire on the cut nerve and the other on a whole nerve, the needle on the new galvanometer moved. He had found the animal electricity, the spirit, the nerve force.

Professor Johannes Müller, following his former student's progress with interest, was certain of one thing: no one would ever measure the speed of this nerve impulse. Electricity traveled too fast. Certainly if the newly invented telegraph could send a message 400 miles, about 644 kilometers, in seconds, there would be no way to time an impulse going from brain to leg. He was wrong. Another of his students, Hermann von Helmholtz, found a way to do it. The speed of nerve action of a frog was about 100 feet, or 30 meters, per second. At that rate it would take hours to send telegrams. Why was the speed of electricity in nerves so slow?

Again the answer had to wait for better, more sensitive equipment. Knowing now that the amount of electricity involved in nerve impulses is a thousandth of a volt, it is surprising that the early, inaccurate equipment picked it up at all. And the confusion over speed of electricity in the nerves was due in large measure to the fact that the "animal electricity" was not the kind of electricity that flows into our homes, lighting lights, powering television. It wasn't a stream of electrons flowing continuously.

The nerve electricity turned out to be a matter of chemicals. None of that could be known until accurate microscopes defined the cells that made up the nerves, until there were stains to see the cells and ways to isolate single cells for study.

Sections of the puzzle were locking together, but as has been said in this decade about the state of brain research, no one knows now or knew then how many pieces of the puzzle were on the floor.

4 *The View from the Microscope*

The view from the microscope changed the world. When Robert Hooke put together the first compound microscope in 1665, it was a voyage to inner space as exciting as any probe of Venus.

In thin slices of cork, Hooke saw honeycombed compartments he called cells because they reminded him of the small rows of rooms used by monks at monasteries. Early microscopes were not optically perfect, and images were distorted, often misleading. When the large nerve from the leg of an animal was put under the microscope, one person thought it was filled with a jellylike substance, another saw globs lined up like beads, and another thought the tubes were full of invisible spirits.

It was commonly believed that nerves carried "a very rich and spiritous juice which is drawn all through the nerves in a constant circuit." Sir Isaac Newton, one of science's most brilliant minds, wrote about the "ethereal vibrations" that began in the brain and moved along the nerves to the muscles. He had the right idea considering that in the 1600s vibration was a description as close as anyone could get to a phenomenon unknown as electrical.

Newton's discoveries ushered in the Age of Reason, a label historians put on the years following the Middle Ages, which are also called the Dark Ages.

The sparseness of great scientific discoveries during those Dark Ages made the years of the 1600s and 1700s seem like a tidal wave of science. Biology, especially, leaped ahead except in the area of brain research. Technology had not caught up enough.

Then in 1830, Jan Evangelista Purkinje, a biology professor in Czechoslovakia, invented the microtome, a piece of equipment that could slice a very thin section of tissue for viewing under the microscope. Before that, inaccurate, uneven slices were cut with knives. With this new technique, Purkinje was able to study nerve tissue, and in 1837 he presented the first good description of a nerve cell. Although he could not see the dendrites and axon, he could see that the nerve cell was like all other cells, containing a nucleus and cytoplasm. At last there was something to work with, the simplest structure of the brain, the building block.

During medieval times various diagrams were used by physicians to locate functions of the brain and other parts of the body. The one pictured here is called the "disease man."

(BAKKEN MUSEUM OF ELECTRICITY IN LIFE)

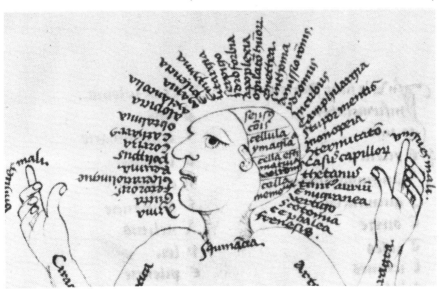

The next important discovery in the field, the discovery many refer to as the single most important step in brain research, was made by an anatomy professor in Italy in 1875. Camillo Golgi was studying the brain tissue of a barn owl. He used the standard techniques to make his microscope slides of the tissue, slicing the sections and staining them with the organic dyes that had recently been discovered in England. But the cells clumped together when stained; he could not see the detail of an individual cell. He began experimenting with silver salts. He went through a long process, hardening the brain tissue in various chemicals and washing them in solutions, including one of silver nitrate, the chemical that turns fingers black in every high school chemistry lab. When he examined the stained tissue under the microscope, he saw a strange thing. Only a few cells had taken the stain, but those few had stained completely. They looked like etchings in black and silver. Instead of a mass of cells, Golgi's stain showed those few neurons with all their branching dendrites and the long kite tail of an axon. He could not explain, nor can anyone now, why or how the stain works as it does.

Scientists had taken sides in a debate over how nerve cells connected. The great majority of scientists were convinced that the nerve cells were connected by an independent network of fibers, a kind of trellis that took impulses from cell to cell. These scientists were called reticulists. (Reticular means netlike.) A smaller number of biologists were called antireticulists. Golgi sided with the more popular reticulists. The anti-reticulists could not prove their case because the stains were still not showing enough. That's when Santiago Ramón y Cajal took the next big step.

Most biological research had taken place in Germany, France, Italy, and England up to this time. Nothing much was happening in America in the field of biology, and certainly no one expected a breakthrough from Spain. Part of science history's fascination with Ramón y Cajal is the fact that he worked in such isolation from other scientists.

"For the biologist, every advance in staining technique is like gaining a new sense with which to explore the unknown," Cajal wrote in his memoirs, and he took Golgi's stain to the next level.

Cajal's father was a well-known doctor, and he fully expected his son to become a doctor. What he did not expect was a son whose only interest was drawing pictures and getting into trouble. When Santiago was eight, he spent so much time drawing that his father finally took the pictures to a local artist who pronounced them terrible. No talent, was the verdict.

With that, Santiago was promptly sent to a school specializing in Latin and Greek. He hated it. He was bored, and it made no sense to him. He was far better at organizing other boys at what he called "pranks." Today we would call him a juvenile delinquent. Teachers punished him constantly. For a while he was locked in a dark room beneath the school, lighted only by a small slit window. Santiago found time to dream in that cell. He found that if he squinted just right, the small window became a kind of telescope. But it didn't stop him from causing trouble all the time.

Next his father sent him to a school where the punishment was starvation. Again in a locked room, Santiago was allowed one meal every twenty-four hours. The scientist Cajal explained that he had three choices: he could pretend to go along with authorities and become a teacher's pet, or he could actually reform and begin to study, or he could continue to fight the system. He fought all the way.

In desperation, his father sent him to serve an apprenticeship with a barber so he would at least have a way to support himself. He was fourteen years old. The barber said, "Take heart, lad. All beginnings are hard."

Next he was apprenticed to a shoemaker. Cajal wrote that his ability to make shoes made "my father more determined than ever to make a Galen of his son." He decided the boy should learn anatomy in case he ever did turn to medicine.

Santiago was amazed when his father took him through the woods one evening to a graveyard where they collected bones for the lessons. His father was equally amazed when just two months later Santiago was able to recite the names of every bone and every bump and dent in each of them. Here at last was a subject he found easy to learn because he could see the objects and handle them. "I was a visual person," he wrote.

His success in anatomy gave him the enthusiasm to finish school. In 1873 he graduated from medical school and enlisted in the Spanish Army Medical Corps. He was sent to a field hospital in Cuba, but he came down with malaria followed by a long bout with tuberculosis. He returned to Spain and graduate school to special-ize in histology, the study of tissue. He was interested in bacteriol-ogy, but he said it required expensive equipment, which he could not afford. But he had a microscope, and that's all he needed for histology.

When Cajal began a task, he did it with a single-minded, unwavering attention. He reported that once he sat at the micro-scope for twenty hours. His drawing skills allowed him to make exquisite illustrations of his microscope slides.

Golgi's stain had been made public in 1880, but few had heard of it or used it. Cajal not only used the stain, but he began to improve upon it.

"The year 1888 arrived, my greatest year, my year of for-tune. From that time on, the trench of science had one more recognized digger," wrote Cajal. "The method of Golgi began to be productive in my hands."

The key to Cajal's success was his decision to "go to the nursery." He said that everyone was looking at the whole forest of cells, or at single trees, but they were not seeing enough, so why not look at the growing tree, the young one? He thought that if he looked at embryonic tissue, cells from unborn birds and mammals, that he would see these nerve cells developing. Golgi had referred to such a method in one of his papers but did not continue it. Cajal found that stain on these developing cells showed with certainty that separate cells communicate with one another over a gap, the synapse. He was also able to show that the cells are not scattered at random but are arranged in incredibly complex interconnec-tions.

Cajal was so anxious to get his discovery to the scientific community, so impatient with the slowness of the usual publica-tions, that he published his own. He mailed out sixty copies. Few scientists saw it, and those who did took little notice of this self-published volume.

Finally Cajal took all his meager savings and traveled to Berlin to an important scientific meeting. He was one of the last speakers at the meeting, but when he presented his theory, a German anatomy professor, Wilhelm von Waldeyer, took notice. He recognized it as a major achievement, and he introduced Cajal to other scientists. They all realized that the Spanish scientist's slides revealed the answer to the reticulist debate. The cells were not on

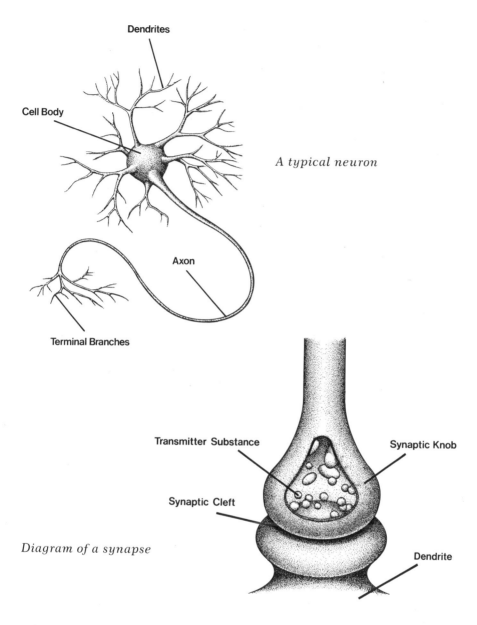

A typical neuron

Diagram of a synapse

a background network or trellis. Waldeyer took credit for coining the word "neuron," but Cajal's greatest contributions were just beginning. He went on to show the direction of flow of nerve impulses from the dendrites through the cell body and out along the axon to the dendrites of the next cell body.

Cajal also believed that nerve cells change as learning occurs. New pathways enlarge, become more involved, expand, and become richer in their number of synapses, but new cells do not appear.

During Cajal's experiments, and in spite of all the publications to the contrary, Golgi clung with determination to his belief in the reticular theory, the network connections. In 1906, Golgi and Ramón y Cajal shared the Nobel Prize in medicine and physiology for their work on nerve cells. The award ceremony was a cold and unfriendly meeting between the two men.

From that time on, neurophysiology, or the study of how nerve cells work, became a major thrust of many laboratories. While some were studying the single cell, however, others were mapping larger territory.

5 *The Map Makers*

When Phineas Gage went to work on the morning of September 14, 1848, he could not guess—nor did he ever know—that he would so greatly influence brain research.

Phineas was foreman of a railroad gang laying line for the Rutland and Burlington Railway near the small town of Cavendish, Vermont. Late in the afternoon they were ready to blast an outcrop of rock. The crew liked their twenty-five-year-old foreman, and they were probably happy to go along with his offer to handle the dangerous job of pouring gunpowder into the deep hole in the rock and tamping it down.

The thirteen-pound (5.8-kilogram) tamping rod was three and a half feet (one meter) long and an inch and a quarter (about three centimeters) in diameter. As Phineas jammed the rod into the hole, metal scraped against rock, and sparks flew and ignited the gunpowder before it was covered by a protective layer of sand.

In the explosion the tamping rod shot like a rocket through Gage's head. It entered just below his left eye, tore through his brain, and emerged from the top of his skull. The rod landed fifty yards (45 meters) away, throwing Phineas Gage in the opposite direction. The foreman's hands and feet twitched in a convulsion, but by the time the stunned crew scrambled to his side, Phineas was able to speak to them.

They loaded him into an oxcart, and although blood was streaming from his wounds, Phineas sat up for the long, jostling ride back to town. At the hotel the wounded man managed to get to a second-floor room, where he waited for the doctor.

Two doctors arrived, and neither could believe the strange story. They were so certain the patient would die that a local cabinetmaker was hired to build a coffin. But by late that evening, Phineas told his friends he would be back at work in a few days.

The wound became infected, and he was delirious with fever for many days. The treatment was castor oil, rhubarb, and calomel tea. Gradually, to everyone's amazement, Phineas improved, and in three weeks he got out of bed and asked for his clothes.

It is interesting enough that the man survived the accident, the infection, and the treatment, but the importance of the story lies in the fact that the friendly, easygoing Phineas had indeed died. The man who now went by that name was described as having "the strength of an ox and an evil temper to match." Phineas was a changed man. The doctor, J. M. Harlow, described him in a medical journal, "In this regard his mind was radically changed, so decidedly that his friends and acquaintances said that he was no longer Gage."

Because of his new, unpleasant personality, he was not hired back by the railroad. He drifted around the country, now and then joining traveling shows to exhibit himself and the tamping rod at county fairs. After his death, his skull and the tamping rod were sent to the museum at Harvard Medical School, where they are still on display.

Gage's accident put into place a piece of the brain puzzle. It showed that a specific part of the brain was responsible for a specific function. Here was Gage walking around with a hole through his brain and acting like a whole man, proof that the front lobe of the brain was not necessary for life.

Today's research is news almost as fast as it happens. A breakthrough in genetic engineering, an experiment on the brain, a probe of Venus, make headlines within hours. The scientists are interviewed on network television, specials are produced, and children read about it in their *Weekly Readers*. But in 1848, the year of Gage's accident, news traveled slowly. People in Cavendish, Ver-

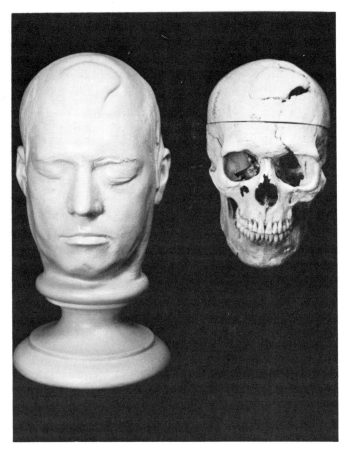

The skull of Phineas Gage shows the almost-healed hole where the tamping rod came out the top of his head, and the cast of his head shows the scar he carried the rest of his life. The thirteen-pound iron tamping rod (below) that passed through his skull is on display at the Warren Museum at Harvard Medical School.

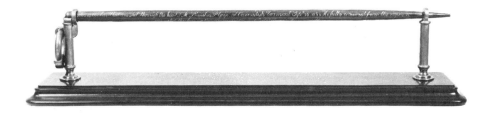

mont, heard of it, of course, and the story passed from person to person—"Did you hear about that foreman fella? Terrible accident. But he lived." The doctors described the case for a medical journal, but publication was a slow process. Several years passed before the article was written, edited, printed, and distributed.

In the year of Gage's accident a new organization started in Paris, a society of "freethinkers." Its founder was Pierre Paul Broca, an unusual man at the time, a man who would be labeled "ahead of his time." He was a surgeon, a neurologist, an anthropologist, and a man concerned with medical care for the poor. He was also a man denounced from pulpits and in newspapers for corrupting young people with new ideas. There are those afraid of new ideas in every age, but in the mid-1880s, anthropology was considered an especially subversive science. Many believed that because man was made in the image of God, one should not question the idea of how or why or when man became man.

Despite the subversive nature of the subject, Broca organized a small group of friends to meet as an anthropology society. In order to hold meetings, Broca was required to get permission from the Minister of Public Instruction and the Prefect of Police. Even then, Broca was warned that he would be held personally responsible for anything said "against society, religion, or the government." As an extra precaution, a plainclothes policeman was assigned to the meetings. The group had no trouble telling which person was the spy, of course. At the first meeting the bored detective wanted to take a break, and he asked Broca to promise not to say anything threatening to the state while he was out. Broca is reported to have said, "No, no, my friend. You must not go for a walk. Sit down and earn your pay."

Broca collected brains. The shelves of his laboratory were lined with jars filled with brains and sometimes whole heads preserved in formaldehyde. He weighed and measured the brains of men, women, and children, looking for similarities and differences. He wanted to know if the brain of an idiot was smaller in size or lighter in weight than that of a brilliant man. Were brains of criminals different from brains of scholars? He wrote dozens of papers comparing sizes and shapes of the brains of apes and men, as well as of man and man.

The discovery that carries his name is of a spot on the brain known as one of the areas responsible for speech. It is on the third convolution of the left frontal lobe of the cerebral cortex, and it is called Broca's area.

Even when Broca had seen eight cases in which injury to the exact spot caused loss of speech, he was reluctant to state it as a proven fact. His notes say, "This number seems to me to be sufficient to give strong presumptions. And the most remarkable thing is that in all the patients the injury was on the left side. I do not dare draw conclusions from this. I await new facts."

Broca was a cautious scientist. He had seen what happened to scientists who got carried away with an idea based on half-truths. Franz Joseph Gall is remembered as a charlatan and a fraud, the originator of a science called phrenology that began in the early years of 1800.

Gall began his career as a doctor in Vienna, where he specialized in the study of the brain and nervous system. He was a people-watcher, and he kept notes describing what he saw. He had noticed that several of his friends had large, protruding eyes, and they also happened to have good memories. Gall thought about this and wondered if protruding eyes were a sign of memory; perhaps other characteristics of personality and ability would show in facial features or shape of skull. He began to measure and plot and chart, collecting evidence for his theory at prisons, insane asylums, and foundling homes. But ". . . phrenology was a bandwagon riding on a bumpy road to scientific disgrace," according to Dr. Colin Blakemore, a physiologist at Cambridge University.

And it was a bandwagon. The new "science" of phrenology, of reading bumps on the head, became a fad. Clinics sprang up offering to read bumps, analyze character, and predict health. Charts were printed and sold. One chart showed 160 labeled squares with everything including a characteristic called Republicanism (no. 149). The wonder is that it took so long to discredit this wrong-way science.

Traces of it hang on today. We still speak of the crest at the base of the skull as the bump of knowledge, and phrenology consultants are found side by side with palmists and spiritualists.

Dr. Gall enjoyed a fashionable following in Vienna until a group of doctors asked him to stop or move away. He moved to Paris, where he lectured at the Institut de France until a committee of its members asked him to stop. The scientists wanted no part of Gall's kind of brain mapping. By the middle of the 1800s they had the evidence of Gage and Broca to point them to an inner mapping of the brain that would far surpass anything they could have imagined. The map of the brain would become so precise that it would be described down to the chemicals that make it work.

A major marking on the brain's map came about as a result of battle injuries. There is nothing good about war, nothing. Some look at medical advances during wartime as an advantage of war; others think it adds a degree of awfulness to know that it takes huge numbers of badly wounded people to spur science on to new treatments. But science does advance in wartime.

In 1870 when the Prussian army captured Napoleon in a battle in northeastern France, two Prussian army doctors treated dozens of soldiers with head wounds. Gustav Fritsch and Eduard Hitzig conducted some experiments on the exposed brains of the injured soldiers. The brain itself feels no pain, and the skull of each man had already been opened. The doctors used fine wires to probe into the brain and stimulate it with small electric currents.

When the back of the patient's brain was touched with the probe, the patient's eyes moved, whether he wanted them to or not. And when the right side of the brain was stimulated, the left side of the body reacted; when the left side of the brain was stimulated, the right side of the body moved.

Fritsch and Hitzig knew they had a marvelous tool for mapping the brain, and they continued their experiments on dogs. The electrostimulation technique became known as ESB. With it, the two Prussian Army medical officers mapped parts of the outer layer of the brain, the cerebral cortex, finding areas of movement, of sight, and of touch. The technique was crude compared to refinements that were to come.

In the 1920s, a Swiss doctor, Walter Hess, probed deeper into the brain when he perfected a way to implant extremely fine electrodes deep into the brains of cats.

Many people express concern about the use of experimental animals. There is no doubt that many animals have suffered so that we can find cures and treatments for the ills of man. Animals are treated more humanely today than in earlier years of biological research because there are laws regulating their use in laboratories. Whenever an animal undergoes surgery, it is with anesthetic. In the case of brain research, once the wound in the skull has healed, the animal can feel nothing implanted in the brain. We use

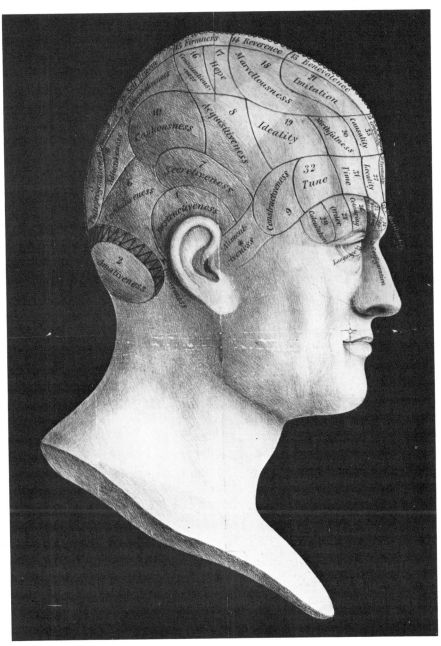

There were many charts for phrenology. The one shown here was devised by Dr. Spurzheim who worked with Dr. Gall. Notice square No. 18 for Marvellousness. (LIBRARY OF CONGRESS)

words and phrases to help us cope with facts. When a loved pet is suffering, we say we have put it to sleep. When deer or other wild animals are killed by conservation officers, we say they are culled or harvested. When research animals are killed after an experiment in order to examine their tissue under a microscope, we say they are sacrificed. We owe a great debt to the millions of animals who have been sacrificed so that we might know how the brain works.

Dr. Hess put the cats to sleep, drilled tiny holes in their skulls, and implanted fine wire electrodes in their brains. When the cats woke up, they seemed not to mind the wires, and they ate and slept and did all the usual cat things.

The electrodes were fully insulated except at the tip so that they would make contact in a precise place. Hess discovered that when he sent a small current through these wires into the hypothalamus, he produced dramatic changes in the animals. A mild-mannered, even-tempered cat suddenly spat and hissed; its ears went back, and the fur on its back rose. It became a frightened cat or an attacking cat. Moved millimeters, the electrodes would stimulate another area that changed the rate of breathing or the blood pressure level. Hess could make the cats eat and eat, even though they were full, or vomit, or sleep. He had discovered the importance of the hypothalamus, the regulator of emotions and the body's internal environment.

As others used the ESB technique to probe man's mind, they discovered things about memory, learning, pain, and pleasure to rival science fiction at its best.

6 *Alpha, Beta, Biofeedback*

"Control your brain waves" may one day be as common as "Please stop talking" is today as a command in a classroom.

As the ESB technique became known for probing deep into the brain, the EEG became known for detecting signals at the surface of the brain. EEG is short for electroencephalogram, a sort of electric head picture. (*Cephalo* comes from the Greek word for head.) It is a test so commonly and painlessly used in hospitals that it is easy to forget that it was a long time in the making.

In the 1870s a physiology professor in England read about the deep probing of dogs' brains done by Fritsch and Hitzig. Richard Caton decided to try to detect brain activity at the surface of the brain. Working with rabbits and monkeys, he was able to pick up feeble currents from electrodes in the skulls of the animals. He found that these currents continued whether the animal was resting or active, and that the currents moved continually back and forth.

When Caton wrote about his experiments, the article was published in a medical journal. Scientists have two methods of telling other scientists what they have done. They go to meetings and present papers describing their experiments, and they publish the results in journals read by other scientists. Before a scientist begins a new series of experiments, he reviews the literature to find out who has been working on what. Caton's article was read by doctors but not by scientists, and it was filed away for fifteen years. Then at the same time three scientists—a Pole, an Austrian, and a Russian—all claimed to have made encephalograms of animals. Caton pulled out his dated article to prove he had done the work first, but another fifty years went by before anyone applied these findings to human brains.

EEGs of human brains were first recorded by an Austrian psychiatrist whose great interest was mental telepathy. Hans Berger was a nineteen-year-old soldier in the German army when he had an accident that changed his life. His horse slipped and plunged them down a cliff. Berger was not seriously injured, but he was surprised to get a telegram the next day from his father asking if he was all right. Just about the time of the accident, Berger's sister had a premonition, a deep feeling that her brother was in danger. Berger was convinced that his sister had picked up a mental message from him, and right then he decided to go back to school to study psychiatry, a field in which he believed he could prove scientifically that mental telepathy did exist. He graduated from the University of Jena in 1897.

It wasn't until 1920 that Berger finally experimented on humans. His first efforts failed because the equipment was not sensitive enough, and Berger didn't know enough about physics and electricity. He was extremely shy, and he could not bring himself to ask for help. It was four years before he finally got results.

Berger's fifteen-year-old son, Klaus, was the guinea pig. He must have been a patient and obedient son to take part in the long series of tests with electrode needles in his scalp. When Klaus was relaxed, but not thinking, the waves being traced on the moving paper were recorded up and down about ten times a second. Berger called these alpha waves. Shorter, more frequent waves appeared when Klaus opened his eyes or read or did any mental work. Berger could tell the moment Klaus began to multiply two numbers and when he stopped. He called these beta waves.

More experiments on people who were asleep or drugged, who had schizophrenia or depression or other mental disorders, showed Berger other waves he called theta and delta. Berger waited five years before publishing his results in scientific journals, and then they were almost ignored. Most scientists of the time were convinced that Berger's results couldn't be true because to record the activity of the whole brain would be too confusing, something like tapping into all the world's phone lines at once. By 1934 two well-respected scientists finally tested Berger's data, and they were so impressed that they suggested calling the alpha waves Berger waves.

Although Berger refused the honor, he was pleased to find himself something of a celebrity outside his native country, then under control of the Nazis. His career ended suddenly one day in September when he received a call from Nazi headquarters ordering him to retire immediately. Twice the Nobel Prize was offered, once before retirement and once after, but both times the Nazis prevented Berger from accepting.

Berger never proved any connection between brain waves and mental telepathy or any other kind of extrasensory activity, but brain-wave reading became almost as much of a fad in Europe as Gall's phrenology had been. Clinics opened where a person could have his mind read, but brain waves did not turn out to be the language of the brain, the code that could be read directly from the mind.

Indirectly, the brain waves are "brain talk." At any given moment a large number of the ten billion neurons are firing in the brain. Although not every cell is sending or receiving at the same time, the brain is constantly active, whether asleep or awake. As long as the brain is alive, some kind of waves appear on the EEG machine. When brain waves flatten out to a straight line, the brain is dead.

Many of the body's organs can be used for transplant if taken from the body immediately after death. In order to protect a dying patient, doctors have agreed to a legal definition of death as that time when there are no brain waves. The heart can be kept beating by machine, the lungs can be worked by a respirator, and the kidneys can function on a dialysis machine, but if no part of the brain is working, the patient is legally dead and the organs can be taken for transplant with the consent of the family or by previous consent of the patient.

Brain waves range from a thousandth to a millionth of a volt. Without the aid of a machine, they cannot be detected.

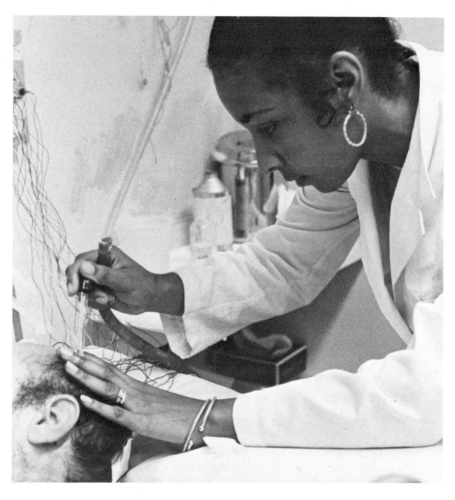

In preparing the patient for an EEG, a technician attaches small wire leads to the scalp with a sticky, salty jell. The wires lead to the machine, which records the brain waves with a moving pen on graph paper.

Today's EEG equipment compares with Berger's the way a supersonic jet compares with the Wright brothers' aircraft. The new EEGs are highly sensitive, computerized machines. Instead of a few needle electrodes stuck into the scalp, today's patient has twenty-one flat metal electrodes glued to the scalp with a salty paste at measured intervals. Just as Berger could tell when his son started to solve a math problem, the EEG operator can tell from the tracings when a person is asleep or only pretending to be, when he is calm or anxious, dreaming or not. The machine can tell when a person is thinking, and at an experimental level, the EEG can predict when a person will make a mistake.

At the Space Biology Laboratory of the Brain Research Institute at UCLA, there is a famous chimpanzee, Jerry, who can play tick-tack-toe. During the hundreds of games Jerry has played with his trainer, his brain waves were recorded. When the scientists analyzed the brain waves by computer, they were able to learn the pattern of brain waves associated with Jerry's correct moves and those that appeared when he made wrong moves. Eventually they were able to watch the EEG printout while Jerry was playing the game and predict when Jerry was going to make a mistake. The scientists were right an amazing 99 percent of the time, and they knew eighteen seconds in advance of the move.

In a conventional electroencephalograph the brain waves are recorded on long sheets of paper while the patient rests in an adjoining room.
(ERIE COUNTY MEDICAL CENTER)

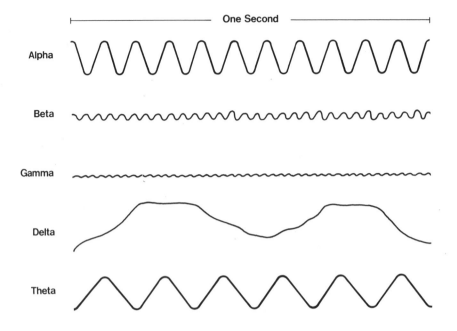

Alpha

Beta

Gamma

Delta

Theta

One Second

Brain-wave patterns as they appear on an EEG machine printout

Of course this is all experimental. The tests are long, painstaking, and extremely far from being put into practice. But imagine what advantages such "errorless learning" would have. An air-traffic controller who can afford no mistakes might wear a helmet fitted with electrodes to record his brain waves. A computer might monitor his waves and set up a warning before he made a wrong decision so that someone else could take over. Someone has suggested such "errorless learning" for a classroom of the future, with students wearing electrodes containing warning lights that would flash when they were about to make a wrong choice. The eighteen-second lead time would allow the teacher, or the teaching machine, to reword the question or rephrase the problem. We know that learning is most effective when the learner is successful, and "errorless learning" would be especially effective.

Dr. Derek Fender, at the California Institute of Technology, learned to analyze brain waves so effectively that he said in an interview with science writer Maya Pines, "You could probably work out a lie detector based on similar principles." Although he has only tried it on a few friends and has not done any long-term research, this scientist has shown he can predict when a person is going to say "yes" or "no." First he identifies the brain-wave pattern associated with the word "yes" and then with "no." Muscle action of the mouth and tongue are different for each word and make different patterns on the EEG. Once a person's pattern is known, the scientist can tell when the person is getting ready to say yes or no even if that person doesn't say it out loud. This is the ultimate in snooping and far from any present use of EEG, of course. In a world where personal freedoms are valued, it isn't likely we will allow the privacy of our thoughts to be taken away.

What is almost as remarkable is the way we can learn to control our own brain waves. Biofeedback is a technique in which

Brain-wave patterns typical of various activities or states of mind   -

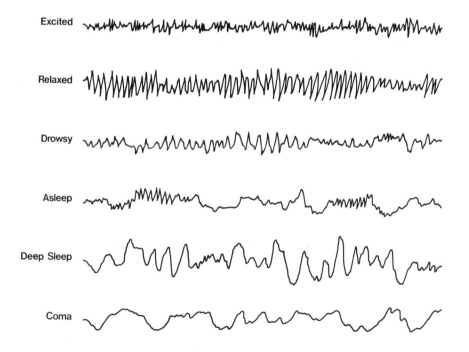

One Second

Excited

Relaxed

Drowsy

Asleep

Deep Sleep

Coma

a person can learn to control breathing, heartbeat, blood pressure, temperature, and other body functions once thought to be involuntary.

Dr. Joseph Kamiya was comparing the brain waves of people asleep and awake when he worked at the University of Chicago in 1958. He wondered if the alpha waves that appear when a person is relaxed could be made to appear on purpose. Could people train themselves to produce alpha waves? As Dr. Berger knew, alpha waves vanish the moment a person opens his eyes, so perhaps these waves could not be ordered up.

The first volunteer for Dr. Kamiya's tests rested in a darkened room with his eyes closed. His brain waves were monitored on an EEG machine in another room. The experimenter rang a bell now and then, and the volunteer was asked to guess whether his brain waves were alpha or beta. The first day the volunteer guessed right about 50 percent of the time, about what is expected by pure chance. The second day he guessed right 65 percent of the time, the third day 85 percent, and on the fourth day he surprised everyone. He guessed right four hundred times in a row. He had learned to recognize his alpha state of mind.

Since then hundreds have tried the experiment. All of them have found the state extremely pleasant and relaxing, but at the same time they were alert. Some called it an "alpha high." They described it as a time of "not thinking" or "letting the mind wander" or "seeing with the mind's eye." All agreed that when they tried to force the feeling or think too hard about it, it didn't work. Thinking produced beta waves.

In the alpha state a person is ready for something to happen. It is a time of attention. A poet told Dr. Kamiya that the alpha state feels like the state he is in just as he gets ready to write a good poem.

The kind of learning done by these volunteers is called biofeedback. We learn many things by this method, getting feedback from eyes, from ears, from teachers, and from other sources to let us know when we're right or wrong. It uses the technique of operant conditioning commonly used in training animals. A pigeon learns to peck at a lever for the instant reward of a food pellet. After a while it can be taught to peck only at the red lever, or to peck five times in a row before the food reward. Dolphins, horses, dogs, and other animals learn like this often with only a pat on the head or a whistle as the reward. Biofeedback uses this same kind of instant reward or reinforcement to let a person know when he has learned to do what the operator wants.

One of the early experiments to see if body functions could be controlled was done on rats. One rat learned to send blood to one ear. The scientist paralyzed the rat with curare, the same poison used on arrow tips by some South American Indians. The rat was immobilized to make sure that the brain, and not any muscles, was controlling reactions. The curare paralyzed the lungs, so the rats were put on tiny rat-sized respirators. The reward was a momentary sensation of pleasure. An electrode had been implanted in the rat's brain so that the probe could reach the "pleasure center," and when the rat succeeded in sending blood to one ear, the operator sent a slight electric impulse to that center. At first the rat was rewarded when it just happened to send blood to one ear, and then it learned how to do this.

Since then people have learned not only to be in the alpha state, but also to raise or lower the temperature in a selected part of the body, to lower blood pressure, or to control an irregular heartbeat. Nothing as drastic as curare needs to be used, of course. A person is fitted with EEG equipment, and a flashing light or beeping signal serves as the reward. To lower blood pressure, for example, a patient wearing a blood-pressure cuff would be alerted by a sound whenever the pressure dropped. He would then try to keep the sound beeping, which would mean the blood pressure was being kept down.

Biofeedback has been called the Zen of the West. Practitioners of Zen and yoga have known for centuries how to control body functions. Mind over matter is not new to them. Eastern yogis can learn to stop bleeding, or to lower the temperature of one hand while raising it in the other, or to control their breathing in order to stay in airtight boxes for hours. Some can walk over coals or lie on a bed of nails.

Mind control is important in all of these feats, but some can be explained by simple laws of physics. Jearl Walker is a superb physics teacher who shows his students how he can walk over hot coals. The main requirement for a fire-walker is enough fear, or at least anxiety, to cause sweating. A thin layer of perspiration on the soles of the feet evaporates, leaving just enough water vapor to protect the feet if you don't loiter. Dr. Walker can lie on a bed of nails because he knows that while one nail would puncture his back, hundreds of nails distribute his weight evenly and support him. It may not be comfortable, but it is possible.

Add to these tricks the composure of a person skilled in meditation, and it is easy to see how these feats are done. But the Zen and Yoga methods of control over breath and blood are not tricks. Without the aid of elaborate electronic equipment like ours, they have learned to do what we are beginning to do with biofeedback.

Many doctors believe that one day biofeedback will be commonly used to help patients control the tremors of Parkinson's disease or the seizures of epilepsy or perhaps even to regulate levels of insulin to treat their own diabetes. Some laboratories are working on biofeedback systems to help amputees operate artificial limbs by signals from the brain. But not everyone is sold on biofeedback.

As fast as legitimate uses are found, some people offer biofeedback as a cure-all, a do-it-yourself miracle treatment. Biofeedback machines for home use are sold and mind-control courses are marketed that guarantee everything from alpha wave control and weight control to personal happiness, more energy, or a higher IQ. Biofeedback requires not only sensitive, expensive equipment but skilled operators, and the home-style version is far from that.

Many scientists are skeptical about brain-wave control. They point out that the brain controls every part of the body, and we have no way of telling how some changes in the brain will change other systems. The language of the brain that Hans Berger hoped would tell us about mental telepathy is still a puzzle. Dr. Kamiya was emphatic when he wrote, in *Psychology Today,* "It must be stressed that there is no connection between alpha waves and extrasensory perception. The amount of energy involved is so infinitesimal that a powerful receiver placed half an inch from the skull could never detect it."

For now the EEG continues to be a good diagnostic tool for brain tumors, blood clots, or other brain damage. Damaged brain tissue sends no messages. No waves, or very slow waves, appear in an area of damage. EEG tests are used to follow the progress of epilepsy to determine what medication should be given. EEGs are inexpensive and useful, but they are being replaced in some cases

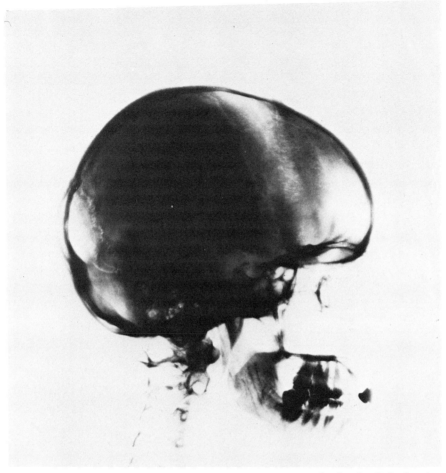

A conventional x-ray of the skull shows a lesion at the back of the brain, but it shows no other details of the brain.

by more sophisticated equipment such as the CAT scanners and the even newer PETT scanners.

The CAT scanner (for computerized axial tomography) takes a series of x-rays that are assembled by computer to give doctors a three-dimensional view of the brain. It can pinpoint the exact site and size of blood clot, tumor, or other damage. (In many hospitals it is referred to as the CT scanner.)

The PETT scanner (for positron emission transaxial tomography), built at the University of Pennsylvania School of Medicine in 1976, probes further. It scans chemically as well as physically.

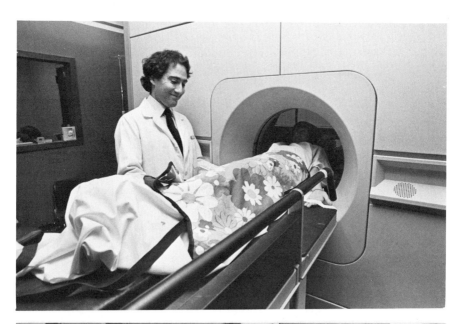

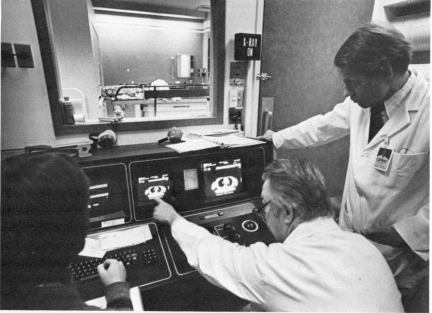

The patient is placed in position for x-rays to be taken by the CAT scan machine (above). *Doctors monitor the screen of the scanner in an adjacent room* (below). (ARTHUR PEASE, PRESBYTERIAN HOSPITAL, COLUMBIA-PRESBYTERIAN MEDICAL CENTER)

48   *The Brain*

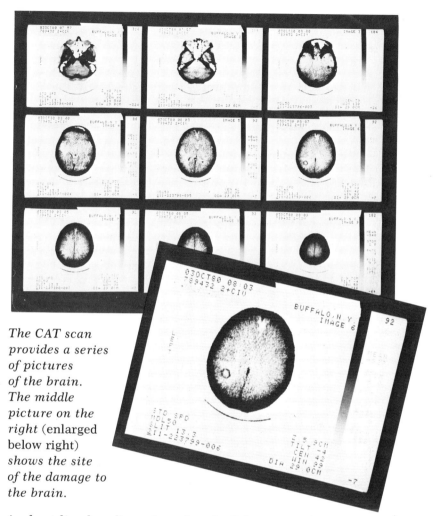

The CAT scan provides a series of pictures of the brain. The middle picture on the right (enlarged below right) *shows the site of the damage to the brain.*

A short-lived radioactive chemical is injected and traced by the PETT so that doctors can diagnose schizophrenia, depression, and other mental disorders. They hope to use it to map the brain in a way never done before. "We don't understand the reasons for everything we're seeing. We only know we're seeing things that no one has ever seen before," Dr. Alfred Wolf, one of the machine's inventors, wrote in *Discover*.

Electronics and chemistry have come together as the sciences that best reveal the biology of the brain. After centuries of thinking of the brain as an electrical machine, it has turned out to be chemical.

7 *The Chemical Connection*

From the time of Galvani's jumping frog-leg experiments, research on nerves and the brain centered around electricity, but always the question remained: *how* did it work? In the end the whole system turned out to be electrochemical, and the clue came once again from a frog.

None of this early research followed a neat, stair-step pattern with one discovery leading directly to the next and the next. One scientist might be working on one aspect that interested him, only to find that his discovery didn't mesh with anything else and so was put on a shelf to wait until it fit into the puzzle. Others worked to a certain level only to find themselves stopped because the technical equipment wasn't sensitive enough or accurate enough to provide all the answers.

The technology of the 1920s brought the radio, and that in turn provided the amplifier scientists needed to pick up and enlarge the tiny amounts of power emitted by a single cell. Although many scientists worked in this area, Lord Edgar Adrian in Cambridge, England, was first to record the nerve impulse on a graph on photographic film. It showed that the nerve impulse moved like a wave in brief bursts that did not change in size but only in frequency. The cell was either on or off, firing or not firing. Again there was a long wait for the next big discovery. Work, however, doesn't stop in laboratories during these periods between big breakthroughs; it is that day-to-day experimentation that makes the breakthroughs possible.

Two things were necessary to measure this wavelike impulse in the neuron: sensitive equipment and a large enough cell. In the development of the cell, nature seems to have hit upon an efficient system of intercellular communication because it hasn't changed much from the lowest order of animals up through man. The same kind of neuron that is present in the human brain is found in cockroaches, crabs, and squids.

By 1937, with equipment for measuring the power of a cell available, several labs found the perfect cell for study. The squid giant axon—not the giant squid, but the giant axon running through the body of a regular small squid—became the star of research. This axon is enormous compared to the largest human neuron.

Scientists at Woods Hole, Massachusetts, and at Plymouth, England, probed with fine silver or platinum wire into this big neuron and measured the electrical difference between the inside and the outside of the cell membrane. The cell membrane had usually been thought of as a container, a sort of bag to hold all the cell's parts. A few scientists in the early 1900s believed the membrane had more important uses, but they had no way to prove it. Now it became apparent that the membrane is very important. The squid axon showed that this wave of "animal electricity" was a wave of electrically charged sodium and potassium atoms (called ions) moving through the cell membrane. The membrane is permeable, which means it allows matter to pass through it. It becomes more or less permeable depending upon the stimulation or lack of it. This electrochemical wave motion explains why the impulse is slow in comparison with the kind of electricity that is a flow of electrons.

When the electron microscope was invented in the 1940s, scientists could see the synapse, that junction where the axon of one neuron meets the dendrites of another neuron. They saw that these parts do not touch. Any leftover reticulists had to concede they were wrong. Between the axon and the dendrites is a tiny gap, also called the synaptic cleft. Sir John Eccles and his team in

Sir John Eccles developed a micropipette with which he explored a single synaptic gap and its functions.
(BUFFALO EVENING NEWS PHOTO)

Australia studied this synapse and gap for more information about the impulse. Eccles devised a micropipette, a hollow glass rod with a tip so small it could be seen only with a microscope.

They gave a cat an anesthetic and opened its skull. With the micropipette filled with salt solution to conduct the electrical impulse, they probed a single neuron. The micropipette was connected to an oscilloscope that gave them a direct reading of the electrical action. They discovered that each cell is assaulted by positive and negative impulses from other cells until one is more powerful than the other and the cell either fires its own impulse down its axon tail or stops the impulse. Each neuron, constantly bombarded by messages from thousands of synapses, must either pass each message along or inhibit it. The next big question was how this impulse gets across the gap. What carries the message?

Meanwhile, in other laboratories during these years of exploring the cell's impulse, others were looking into an old idea that chemical connections were somehow involved in the nervous system.

In the 1920s Dr. Otto Loewi, an Austrian physiologist, had been studying nerve fibers. One night he was mulling over ideas for an experiment. He had trouble getting to sleep, tossing and turning until three in the morning, when he had a great idea. He wrote it down as fast as he could, then went to sleep. The next morning, eager to get to work, Loewi found that he couldn't read what he had scribbled in his bedside notebook. The next night he awoke again with the idea, but this time he got up, dressed, and hurried to his lab. By dawn he had completed the experiment.

Loewi removed fluid from the vagus nerve of one frog and injected it into the heart of another frog. The vagus nerve is one of the nerves that regulates heartbeat. This substance stimulated the heart of the second frog. Loewi didn't know what the chemical was so he called it vagusstoff (vagus material). Although he did not realize it, he had found the first neurotransmitter, the first chemical messenger.

Another piece of this puzzle started to fall into place ten years before Loewi's work. In 1910, Sir Henry Dale had been experimenting with a fungus called ergot. He isolated a substance he called acetylcholine. It could make a muscle contract just as an electric shock could, but he wasn't sure how it worked. He put it aside and studied other things. Twenty years later Dale read about the vagusstoff, and it sounded to him just like his acetylcholine. He wondered if he could find it in animals as well as in fungus.

Dale and his team went to a slaughterhouse and collected seventy-one pounds (157 kilograms) of spleens from twenty-four horses. When the spleens were reduced and filtered, he had all of 334 milligrams of acetylcholine, but it was enough to prove that it was the same chemical as vagusstoff. Now the first of the chemical messengers had a name, but still they did not know it exactly as a messenger. The synaptic gap had not been seen. Dale and Loewi shared the Nobel Prize in 1936 for their work.

Two years later Loewi was arrested in Nazi-held Austria because he was Jewish. Afraid he was going to be killed, Loewi persuaded a friendly guard to mail a postcard for him to a scientific journal. He thought it might be his last chance to explain his work. Fortunately, Loewi lived, but he had to turn over his Nobel Prize-money to the Nazis before they allowed him to leave the country. In 1946 he became an American citizen and continued to work on brain chemistry.

The knowledge of Loewi's and Dale's chemical transmitter spread rapidly to other labs, and a barrage of studies was started to find other transmitters. After acetylcholine, a neurotransmitter called noradrenaline was isolated. Now we know of two dozen transmitters with names like dopamine, serotonin, tyramine, enkephalin, and a substance P, named because it was found in a powder. There may be unknown hundreds more.

When the electrical impulse reaches the end of the axon, the neurotransmitters are released from their storage vesicles. They cross the synaptic gap and link to receptor sites on the next neuron. It is a specific lock-and-key arrangement with a perfect-fit receptor for each neurotransmitter. There are two kinds of keys for these receptor locks. One is called excitatory because it excites, or starts the action of, the impulse in the receiver neuron. The other is called inhibitory because it stops the firing of the neuron. The chance of one neuron firing depends upon the sum total of these stop or go messages. If there are five excitatory neurotransmitters, they could be counteracted by more of the inhibitory transmitters. With thousands of these lock-and-key almost-connections on every one of the ten billion neurons, the brain is in constant action. This is why brain waves are recorded, awake or asleep, until a person is dead.

Changes in the levels of these neurochemicals can cause trouble. Mental illnesses such as schizophrenia and manic-depression are now thought to be caused by changes in the chemistry of the brain. Alcoholism and drug addiction are now regarded as problems caused by look-alike intruders taking over the receptor sites of neurotransmitters.

By the 1970s the great race was on to find these lock-and-key arrangements, to discover more neurotransmitters, and to figure out what they do. Each step was more amazing than the last. It was like opening the world's most enormous surprise package, and one of the biggest surprises was finding the opiate of the mind. Why did the human brain have in it receptor sites for the juice of the poppy?

8 *The Drug Machine*

Endorphin . . . it sounds like a word made up by an ad agency to sell nose drops, or perhaps the name of one of the Hobbits, but it is a combination of Greek words that mean "the morphine within." The discovery of endorphins, the drugs within our own brains, was a breakthrough in science more exciting than the discovery of insulin or even antibiotics. It may prove to be the key to curing drug addiction, to healing mental illness, to controlling pain, and to understanding the delicate balance that maintains a "normal" brain.

Endorphins are a group of narcotics manufactured by the brain and the pituitary gland, and they act like opium, morphine, and heroin. They belong to a family of compounds called peptides, which are short chains of amino acids.

A long time before the chemistry of the brain was known, there were clues that suggested to scientists the presence of some kind of automatic pain control in the body. Why was it, for example, that soldiers horribly wounded in battle would at first be almost oblivious to the pain? Was it merely shock, or was there some way in which the body blocked the pain? And why did acupuncture work? For centuries the Chinese inserted thin acupuncture needles at prescribed points on the body to relieve pain to a degree that allowed even major surgery. Western doctors suggested that acupuncture must be partly hypnotism, but Oriental doctors point out that acupuncture works in emergency situations when there is no time for hypnotism. All these things pointed to the presence of some painkiller within.

During the 1970s millions of dollars in federal grants were given to laboratories to find out why people became addicted to drugs and how they could be helped. At this time two lines of research came together. In the 1950s and 1960s, about half of the schizophrenic patients in mental hospitals were "cured" of their disturbing symptoms because of two powerful new drugs. One was chlorpromazine, a tranquilizer, and the other was amphetamine, which was just the opposite. It produced a speeded-up reaction called a "high."

The research on the neurotransmitters showed that chlorpromazine blocked the neurotransmitter called dopamine, thereby slowing down the action along pathways involved in emotions. They knew also that amphetamines released large amounts of a neurotransmitter called epinephrine, thereby speeding up the signals between neurons.

For a long while these two drugs were believed to be the answer to mental illness. They certainly were superior to the earlier treatment of mental patients. The drugs alone can produce symptoms exactly like schizophrenia or depression, however, so they must be carefully controlled. But one great problem remained. If these drugs were the answer, why were there still some 330,000 patients who did not respond to the treatments?

Something was missing. It meant they had found a medication, but not the original cause. Interviewed for a 1978 *Atlantic Monthly* article, Dr. Floyd Bloom at the Salk Institute in San Francisco said, "The time had come to begin taking the things the brain had stored on its shelves down, one by one, and start looking at them very closely."

Labs everywhere took up the search. Avram Goldstein at the Stanford Addiction Research Center suggested looking for a receptor site for drugs in the membranes of the nerve cells. He knew that morphine is inert, which means it doesn't do anything by itself. It must react with something, and Goldstein thought there must be a place in the brain where this drug might fit in a

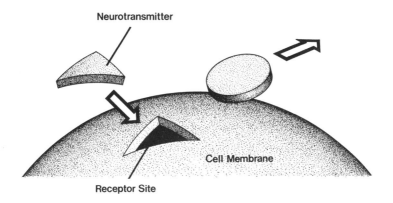

Neurotransmitter

Cell Membrane

Receptor Site

Diagram of a receptor site on a cell membrane. Only the right "key" will fit into the receptor "keyhole."

lock-and-key arrangement like the neurotransmitters. But where? It was like searching for a single keyhole in an entire city.

When a drug addict enters an emergency room in a coma, the doctors give him an injection of a morphinelike substance called naloxone. It acts so fast that often the patient begins to come out of the coma before the needle is out of his arm. Naloxone is a morphine antagonist. That means that it fits in morphine's receptor site so well that it keeps morphine molecules out. It is as though someone had a key to your house so exactly like the real key that he could open the door, and when that key was in the lock, your key couldn't fit in.

This naloxone fits in morphine's receptor site, but it doesn't trigger the same kind of chemical action that produces the morphine "high." It can't be used for a painkiller, however, because its effects last a very short time. The labs decided to use naloxone as a way to test for receptor sites. They reasoned that if the action of an unknown drug in the brain can be reversed by naloxone, it must be very much like morphine.

They injected rats' brains with naloxone "tagged" with a short-lived radioactive glucose. The radioactive material could be traced, and it would not interfere with the chemical action they were seeking. When they killed the rats and removed the brains, they were able to separate the parts of the nerve cells "tagged" by the radioactive material and thereby locate the receptors. This is done by homogenizing the rat brains to a thin-soup consistency and then spinning that soup in a centrifuge to extract cells. The radioactive molecules bound tightly to the cell fragments remain in the test tubes after a washing technique.

In 1973 Dr. Candace Pert found the receptor sites. "I'd tried and tried and tried and gotten nothing," she reported in the *Atlantic Monthly,* "and then one day . . . there they were. I was looking at something in the brain nobody had ever really known was there before." Dr. Pert was working with Dr. Solomon Snyder at Johns Hopkins as a graduate student at the time. She had started the washing technique on a Friday, then left the lab, leaving it to run all weekend. Her very thorough washing worked.

At the same time Dr. Eric Solomon at New York University and another group, under the direction of Dr. Lars Terenius at the University of Uppsala in Sweden, made the same discovery only a few weeks later. The receptor sites were mostly concentrated in the parts of the brain known to send signals of chronic pain, and they were also deep in the limbic system where emotions are controlled.

Candace Pert continued tests on other animals, and strangely enough she found these same receptors in the hagfish, an animal whose ancestors lived 350 million years ago in the Devonian seas. Why would there be a receptor site in the brain of the hagfish for the juice of the poppy flower? It didn't make sense unless all animals had a system of coping with pain, and that system made use of something resembling morphine. Nature is too efficient to build unnecessary systems. A collector in Texas sent Dr. Pert a batch of tarantulas, and she repeated the tests with the spiders' brains. Spiders, she found, do not have receptor sites for the drugs. Could it be that invertebrates, the lower forms of animals, feel no pain and do not have a need for such receptors? No one knows for sure, but it seems to be the case.

With proof of a receptor site for a morphinelike substance, scientists raced to find the substance itself. With proof of the keyhole, they knew there must be a key, a narcotic made by the brain. Three labs led the race, one in Scotland, one in Sweden, and one in the United States.

Research is a team game, but someone always scores the winning goal. In the *Atlantic Monthly* article, Avram Goldstein pointed out that "science is just that, a race. It's cooperative,

Dr. Candace Pert, now an independent researcher at the National Institutes of Mental Health, discovered the receptor sites in the neurons when she was a graduate student with Dr. Snyder at Johns Hopkins University.
(CANDACE PERT)

but it's competitive too, and probably more of the latter because scientists are by nature competitive people."

Solomon Snyder at Johns Hopkins, Hans Kosterlitz and John Hughes at the University of Aberdeen in Scotland, and Lars Terenius in Sweden were the main contenders. In 1973 Terenius visited Scotland, and he told Kosterlitz that he thought they were going to find that the morphinelike molecule would be big, but Kosterlitz was convinced it would be a small molecule, like morphine itself.

In 1974 both the Scotland and Sweden labs found a big molecule. America was behind in the race. Hughes and Kosterlitz isolated two opiate peptides from pigs' brains, and they called these enkephalins. A few weeks later, Snyder in his lab at Johns Hopkins confirmed this discovery using calves' brains. Snyder's team went on to map the relationship between these two enkephalins and their receptor sites that Candace Pert had found earlier.

There are two kinds of pain, slow and fast. The fast pain travels by express, making few stops on its way to the brain. It's the kind of pain felt instantly, as when you step on a tack or prick your finger. Slow pain can make many stops and starts. There is no precisely localized spot, but rather a throbbing, lingering, more generalized pain. This pain pathway is also responsible for our reaction to pain such as panic, fright, or depression. Snyder's lab found that the cerebral cortex, the roof-brain, has almost no opiate receptors. Pain is not controlled by the thinking part of the brain. Instead, the majority of these enkephalin receptors are found exactly where the sites of pain and emotions had been mapped by electrodes. Deep within the brain, in the doughnut-shaped limbic system, were high concentrations of the receptors in the slow-pain pathway. This is why morphine can soothe the anxiety of a cancer patient as well as ease the pain. The location of these receptors in this part of the brain that also controls emotions made it seem likely that any unbalance in these messenger-molecules could make a person emotionally disturbed.

Ten years before the discovery of the enkephalins, Dr. Choh Hao Li at the University of California at San Francisco had found a hormone without a function. He had isolated a peptide from the pituitary gland of sheep that he called beta lipotropin, but he couldn't find out what it did. He put it back on the shelf and forgot about it until he got a phone call from Avram Goldstein in 1974. Goldstein called to tell him about the enkephalins, and he read the chemical sequences to Li over the phone. It was the same peptide Li had found in the sheep pituitary.

Li decided to explore his discovery further. At that time he had a graduate student from Iraq, and they both wondered if this beta lipotropin would be found in camels as well as sheep. Camels are tough and thin, and they don't seem to react to pain even if you stick a knife in them. Would they have a different pain chemical than sheep? When his graduate student returned to Iraq, he sent Dr. Li two hundred camel pituitaries.

Dr. Li found a new, smaller hormone in the camel, and he called it beta endorphin. "When Goldstein called and told me beta lipotropin contained the enkephalins, I knew my camel material must be very active. I let him test it and it was," said Li. Li sent some of the beta endorphin to several other laboratories, where it was also found in the pituitaries of monkeys and other test animals. The endorphin was found to be one hundred times more potent than morphine, and about forty times more effective as a painkiller than the enkephalins when it was injected into the brains of test animals.

Dr. Li began to make human beta endorphin in his lab, and by 1977 he had enough to give to three other scientists to test on humans. With an FDA license to go ahead, they tested it on patients with extreme chronic pain, on patients trying to withdraw from heroin addiction, and on some patients with different kinds of mental illness. The results were exciting.

One schizophrenic patient had no more hallucinations and reported feeling "right" again, as he had years before his illness. It worked on the addiction, on the mental illness, and on the pain. It was horribly expensive, costing about $3,000 per injection. "But think of what it may mean when we get costs down!" said one of the researchers. "We've certainly pushed open the door to a fascinating new era of research."

If endorphin therapy works, drug addiction may one day be only an awful memory. It may be that addicts take drugs to overcome inborn endorphin deficiencies.

Although it happens rarely, there are people born with no ability to feel pain. An extreme case was that of F.C., the daughter of a Canadian doctor. This girl was so completely insensitive to pain that she chewed the tip of her tongue to a pulp without knowing it. She kneeled on a floor heat register and burned her legs badly. When she dislocated both shoulders, she felt no pain when they were replaced. Now it is believed she had an endorphin imbalance, perhaps an overload.

Later investigations split the beta endorphin into two separate endorphins called alpha and gamma. Though they differ by only one amino acid, they have quite opposite effects. The alpha endorphin, like the enkephalins, tranquilizes and stops pain. The gamma endorphin, when tested on animals, produced reactions of violence, irritability, and a super-sensitivity to pain.

A badly wounded person may not feel the pain at first because of a surge of his own narcotic. One scientist speculated that perhaps a hero is simply a person with a large amount of endorphin, while a coward who breaks under torture may have a low supply of his own narcotic. Or there may be a larger supply of gamma endorphin manufactured in one situation, alpha in another. Tests have shown that acupuncture does stimulate the body's endorphins, setting up a pain barrier when the needle is inserted.

Endorphins have been found in the amniotic fluid, the liquid that supports and surrounds the baby as it grows in the mother. A baby floating in this natural opiate is relaxed, sleepy, and calm. "It's fascinating to think about the fetus in this blissful prenatal state medicated by beta endorphin," said Dr. Pert. It was she and her husband, Agu Pert, both now in research at the National Institutes of Mental Health, who discovered the endorphin in the fluid. They also believe that a mother produces more endorphins when she begins labor.

Shortly after the discovery of the amino-acid sequence of enkephalin, drug companies began to make a version of the natural drug. Since it is the brain's own morphine, they hope the new drug will not be addictive and that it will improve mood as well as kill pain. Other brain-made drugs have been discovered. Susan Leeman, at Harvard, discovered a peptide called neurotensin, which is more potent than the enkephalins, and drug companies would like to develop that into a super pain pill.

More and more of these brain chemicals will probably be isolated. The endorphin discovery was a complete reversal of the usual experiments. Instead of trying to develop drugs that mimic brain action, familiar drugs, like morphine, were used as the model to find the brain chemical. It was not an accidental discovery, but rather a systematic, logical inquiry based on what was known about narcotic drugs.

9
Just Remember This

Pop a pill and remember the American history lesson or recall the algebra? Take the right chemical at the right time, and studying will be a thing of the past? Don't count on it. We are learning how we learn, how we store and retrieve memories, but there are more theories than facts at this point.

Memory is certainly the biggest puzzle of the brain. How in that three pounds (1.35 kilograms) of cells can a person store more facts and impressions than there are words in any set of encyclopedias? For years the search was on for an engram, or trace, some physical change in the neuron. At first science looked to the electrical nature of the cell for this engram, but now the evidence is strong for a chemical code.

There are three kinds of memories: long-term, short-term, and ancestral. Ancestral memory is in our genes. It is the kind of memory we call instinct in animals, the kind of memory an animal possesses without learning. A beaver raised alone in a concrete pool in a zoo knows how to build a dam or cut a tree beaver-style if it is returned to a stream. Uninstructed, a bird knows how to build a nest. A human baby is born knowing how to suck, to cry when hungry. We have inborn gestures and behaviors from our ancestral, built-in memory. Our tendency to have a leader for the group (family, country, business), the way we greet each other with nods, back slaps, hugs, the way the hair on the back of the neck prickles when we are afraid, all are built-in memories from a long line of ancestors.

We can lose short-term memories while keeping long-term memories, or the other way around. H.M. is as famous in brain studies as Phineas Gage. H.M. cannot remember what he did a moment ago. Always referred to by his initials to protect his privacy, H.M. was a patient with severe epilepsy. Several times a day he was thrown into convulsions, so that doctors decided to operate to try to stop these brainstorms of misfiring neurons. In 1953, surgeons removed parts of the temporal lobes of the cerebral cortex, the areas on either side of the head above the ears. Unfortunately, they also cut the hippocampus, a sea horse–shaped section about three centimeters (one inch) long buried under the lobes. The surgeons have urged others never to repeat the operation because of the disastrous results.

H.M. recovered and feels fine, except he can't remember what he did just a few minutes ago. He has one copy of an old magazine that he reads over and over because it is always new to him. He cannot go outside alone because he would get lost. He can remember the route to his childhood home, where he lived before his surgery, but not the way to get to his present home. He is always apologizing because he can't remember what he has done. Did he offend anyone? Was he rude? Did he meet you before?

The place where short-term memories are apparently stored is gone in H.M. But once he surprised the doctor by showing him a 1968 Kennedy half dollar, made fifteen years after his operation, and telling the doctor who Kennedy was and that he had been assassinated. Is some part of H.M.'s brain beginning to take over the job of the severed hippocampus? Nobody knows.

Most of what we know about memory storage comes from goldfish, gerbils, rats, and flatworms. In computer language, the steps of memory-making are described as input, storage, and readout. They are also called the three Rs—registration, retention, and recall—although some add a fourth R, recognition. Recognition is the sense of familiarity, the ability of the brain to recognize a person a block away even though his face cannot be seen, to recognize a place from the clue of a sound or a silhouette of a skyline, or to know a song from a few notes.

Karl Lashley found where memory is *not.* Almost his entire career up through the 1950s was devoted to training rats to learn simple actions, such as finding their way through mazes, and then removing parts of their brains. When a rat recovered from the operation, it was sent through the maze to see what it remembered. Lashley was amazed to discover that he could cut away almost 90 percent of the brain before the rat "forgot" everything. Toward the end of his career, Lashley expressed his never-ceasing wonder when he thought about finding the place of memory in the brain. He expressed his amazement that it was possible to learn at all.

But of course it is possible, and others have kept searching for the key. When Wilder Penfield, a Canadian neurosurgeon, was operating on epileptic patients in an effort to cut down on severe seizures, he found areas of the brain involved in memory.

Patients were conscious during the surgery in order to tell Penfield when he had touched the right spot. The scalp and skull were opened under local anesthetic and the brain was exposed. The brain itself feels no pain, so Penfield was able to probe without any discomfort to the patient.

He was hoping to find the spot that causes what is known as an aura, a kind of warning sense that comes before an epileptic attack. Penfield tested many areas. When he touched the motor cortex, the patient's muscles jumped. When he touched the visual cortex, the patient saw flashes of light and swirling colors. But then he touched a spot on the hippocampus, the sea horse–shaped section that had been destroyed in H.M., and Penfield found not just a memory but a reliving of an event. The patient was fully aware of being in an operating room, but at the same time seemed to be in the middle of an event from the past. One young woman patient said, "I think I heard a mother calling her little boy . . . in the neighborhood where I lived."

Another young woman patient heard an orchestra playing so clearly that she thought there was a radio in the operating room. She hummed along with it whenever Penfield applied the electrode to one spot, but she stopped when he removed it.

Another patient, a twelve-year-old boy, suddenly said, "Oh, gosh, there they are, my brother is there," when Penfield stimulated his brain. All of the patients reported the event as more real than just memory. They felt as though they were in the midst of it. It was happening again. Penfield had found sites of stored memories, but still no trace, no engram, no explanation for *how* those memories are stored or retrieved.

In a series of experiments at the University of California at Berkeley, rats were separated into two groups. One group was active. Trained to do simple things, they were kept in an area where they could poke around and explore. The other group was kept more isolated, in regular, dull rat cages with nothing to do but eat and sleep. When the brains of these rats were compared, it was found that the cerebral cortex of the rats who had been active and learned were larger than those of the do-nothing rats. The active rats had experienced things that presumably made the brain bigger. Here was some physical evidence of learning. Could it be that changes occur in the neuron? Could there be a memory molecule? Some scientists looked to RNA (ribonucleic acid), the material that transfers the genetic memory, and others bet on proteins as the memory vehicle.

Then a series of tests on flatworms set off a wave of arguments that still go on. Dr. James McConnell at the University of Michigan trained some flatworms called planaria, one of the simplest animals with a brain and synapse. He taught them to crawl toward a light whenever they received a mild shock. When they had learned this, McConnell cut the worms in half. Planaria regenerate, or grow new parts, the way a lizard grows a new tail. When all the heads had grown new tails, the animals were tested, and they remembered to go toward the light. Then McConnell tested the tails that had grown new heads. Somewhere in the nerve fiber of the "educated" worm was the memory because even the planaria with new heads remembered.

Next he chopped up the trained planaria into little pieces and fed them to untrained worms. To his delight, McConnell reported in Calder's book, *The Mind of Man*, the cannibals that had eaten the educated victims did better in the tests than did cannibals that had eaten untrained worms. He called it a transfer of information. Immediately, other laboratories tried, with little success, to duplicate the experiment to see if it was really possible to swallow memories. Few believed it could be done, and arguments flew.

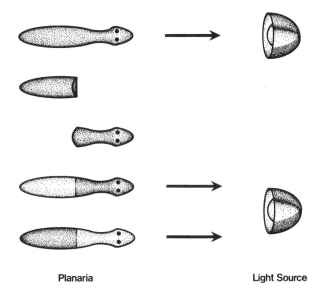

Planaria   **Light Source**

A planaria was taught to move toward light. It was cut in half, and when each half regenerated, the new animals seemed to retain the memory of the move toward light.

Next, it was tried with rats. Planaria could "swallow" their information, but rats, as well as man and other mammals, have digestive juices that would destroy the chemicals. The rats would have to be injected instead. In this experiment, rats were taught to perform certain tasks and then were killed. The RNA taken from the trained rats' brains was injected into the brains of untrained rats. There was evidence that the rats injected with their dead brothers' information were able to learn the same tasks more quickly than those that didn't get the injection.

For a while a lot of people were excited about the idea of learning by injection, of taking a pill to improve memory. Others said there were too many factors unaccounted for, and that line of research has little support now.

Dr. Georges Ungar in Houston, Texas, had the spotlight on his laboratory when he found a chemical of learning. Rats normally like to find dark holes, places where they can hide and feel safe. Ungar taught rats to be afraid of the dark by giving them a shock every time they went into the dark box. When those rats were

Just Remember This   67

killed and the extracts from their brains were injected into unafraid rats, they, too, became afraid of the dark. It was a chemical in the brain Dr. Ungar called scotophobin, from the Greek word *skotos* for darkness, and *phobos* meaning fear.

Laboratories everywhere in the 1960s and '70s pushed to find the key to learning and memory. In another lab at the University of Michigan, Dr. Bernard Agranoff taught goldfish to swim over tiny hurdles in their individual tanks toward a light and away from an electric shock. It doesn't take a fish long to learn this, but when Dr. Agranoff injected a drug called puromycin into the heads of the goldfish, the fish forgot what they had learned. Puromycin is an antibiotic that is known to reduce the rate of protein manufactured in the brain. When this drug erased the memory in the fish, it was interpreted that protein was a vital part of memory.

When a fish was injected immediately after training, it would forget, but if an hour passed before the injection, the fish's memory for the training remained. The experiments seemed to be evidence that chemical changes occur in forming long-term memory. But others felt that the drug injected may have only temporarily poisoned the brain or impaired it the way a blow on the head can temporarily dislodge memory.

Most machines break down when a part breaks, but the brain is a reliable machine made up of unreliable parts. When some of the cells of the brain stop working, the brain continues to work. Nature created this system by using more than one part to do a particular job. It is described as redundancy. A redundancy is an excess, a superabundance. It is redundant to say "very excellent" because "excellent" alone means the best, and it is an excess of words to add the "very." It is redundant to say a white polar bear because all polar bears are white.

It is this redundancy of brain functions that made some of the old ideas of brain maps out of date. How could a rat lose 90 percent of its brain and still remember? In an interview in *Psychology Today*, Karl Pribram said, "If a person has a stroke and half his brain is destroyed, he doesn't come home and recognize only half his family." His experiments showed that if only 2 percent of a particular system in the brain is working, the whole system works. Imagine if 98 percent of the kidneys were gone and the other 2 percent worked so well you never knew the rest was gone.

Brain researchers agree that memory results from biochemical changes stored in individual cells that can be electrochemically activated. The search was always for the engram, the change in the cells that marked a memory, but it never explained how different sets of cells had the same information.

Pribram asked himself how we can recognize an object, regardless of how far away it is or from what angle we view it. How do we recognize a person seen one time face to face and at another time from a second-story window? How are skills transferred? If something goes wrong with a person's right hand, he can learn—slowly perhaps, but he can learn—to write with the left hand, or with the pencil between his teeth, or even between his toes. "Something has happened that takes memory of my learning how to write and distributes it to places in the brain where it's never been called on before," says Pribram.

Karl Pribram offers the theory of the hologram. It's an unproven idea, but it makes such sense that it is under intense investigation. It explains the redundancy of memory storage.

A hologram is a three-dimensional photograph taken with the polarized light of a laser. Light waves can best be compared to people. If you stand on a corner of a busy intersection and watch people, you see all shapes and sizes of people moving at different speeds—ambling, walking, jogging, running. Light waves are like those people, all sizes moving at varying speeds.

A laser produces light that is more like a group of clones, people of identical shape and size, walking close together in cadence, not varying a beat. Laser light waves move at one speed, on one plane, with no variation. Holograms are made with this orderly, pure light source.

If you drop two pebbles into a pond, the ripples from each will run into each other at a point called the interference pattern. Two laser beams sent out meet and produce an interference pattern of light and dark. If one beam is reflected off a face and then strikes a photographic plate, the plate will record the interference pattern and store the image of that face. In ordinary light, the plate looks gray, but when light from a projector hits it, the original interference pattern creates a three-dimensional image called a hologram.

Pribram believes that the brain stores memories from sensory input in interference patterns. He thinks the "situational clues" for memory are sets of wave forms that can activate the appropriate hologram. It explains many things, including how we learn by imitation. Pribram asks us to imagine what it would be like to learn a tennis serve if you had to describe every move to yourself, feature by feature. "You never think about doing it that way . . . you just watch how it's done, then go ahead and try it yourself." What happens is that the brain receives a set of wave forms encoded in the movement, and then it sets up similar wave forms to carry out the tennis serve. "In a sense," says Pribram, "we resonate to vibrations; we actually can resonate to each other's 'vibes.' "

He continues, "One of the elegant things about holographic domain is that memory storage is fantastically great. Storage is also simpler because all that is needed is to store a few rules rather than vast amount of detail."

A hologram compares with a regular photograph the way a three-dimensional doll compares with a paper doll. You can walk around it and see not just the imprint of the paper company, but the back of the image. When you cut up a photograph you get scraps. When you cut up a holographic plate you still have the whole picture. It is similar to looking through a window that has been blacked out except for a single spot; you can see the whole scene, but from that one spot. If you're looking at a tree, you might see it from the top, or only the trunk, or one side, but you recognize it as a tree. The angle changes.

With holographic memory we recall information from different angles, different clues. For example, the smell of bread baking might trigger the memory of your grandmother's kitchen or a street you walked down one day.

We remember in chunks, so chunking information together is a good technique for learning and remembering. Rote memory is the least effective. Learning a list of definitions or spelling words or dates might stay in the mind long enough to get through one quiz. But if it is chunked together in groups, it is more lasting. We tend to remember best by association, so that we remember names by connecting them to an idea or an object. We can mentally see Mr. Lyon in a cage, Miss Pratt falling on her face. The associations provide more clues to call upon from the memory storage.

We seem to remember best in the place where we learned it. If you learn math in room 114, it's harder to take the final exam in the school cafeteria because the associations aren't there. If you run upstairs to get something and stand there wondering what it was you wanted, you go back downstairs, stand a minute, and some association will bring it to mind. The more clues you have, the more likely you are to remember. Bits and pieces, chunks of interference patterns, meet constantly in the brain, retrieving information for us. The cortex looks for the answers from previously learned information and uses combinations or different applications of what has been stored. New learning can erase old information as taping new sounds erases old ones on the tape. We abort old programs, let them go, and replace them with new combinations.

We know a lot about the brain now compared with the early days of brain research, and still we know nothing. We have hints, clues, theories, but still the question remains: How do we think? How does the mind remember, and love, and what makes us laugh? What combination of chemicals does all this, or will we find the chemicals and still not know the *how* of it?

10 *Right Brain, Left Brain*

"I have half a mind to do it."

"His right hand doesn't know what his left hand is doing."

"I can't think of a word for it, but I can see it in my mind's eye."

"On one hand . . . and on the other hand . . ."

"I'm of two minds on that matter."

We are indeed of two minds. We can see things in our mind's eye, although we can't think of words to describe them. Some people express things well in words but are all thumbs when they try to hit a nail with a hammer or knit a sweater. Others can draw a diagram to explain an idea or paint a watercolor with ease, although they find it agonizing to write a business letter.

Clichés about two-mindedness abound, but they are rooted in biological fact. The brain uses a crossover system. The right side of the brain controls the left side of the body, and the left side of the brain controls the right side of the body. Although the two halves of the cerebrum, the roof-brain, work side by side, each specializes in a different set of functions. Each of us has a tendency to be either right-brained or left-brained. Until the experiments on split-brain patients in the 1960s, not much was known about the separate halves.

In the mapping of the brain, one section remained uncharted territory. The thick chunk of nerve fiber that connects the left and right cerebral hemispheres is called the corpus callosum, and no one could find what it was for. It seemed to serve no purpose. In a series of experiments on cats, their corpus callosa were severed, and when they recovered from the surgery, the cats ate, slept, walked, and generally behaved like normal cats. One scientist said, only a bit facetiously, that maybe the corpus callosum was there just to keep the two halves of the brain from sagging.

Experiments continued, first on cats and then on dogs, monkeys, and chimpanzees. The selection of shapes taught to the split-brain animals were remembered only by the side of the brain that learned it, so that if a chimp saw a square with the right eye (left brain), he could not recognize it with the left eye only (right brain). After many complex experiments, it was finally clear that the corpus callosum must be the bridge that carries information from one side of the brain to the other.

The thorn in the side of this study on animal brains was the fact that both sides of animal brains are alike. Man is the only animal in which the halves of the brain are assigned different jobs. There was no way to experiment on humans until a now famous operation was performed on a man listed in the journals as W.J.

W.J. had been hit by shell fragments in World War II, and some of these metal fragments were embedded in his brain. After a few years, the brain reacted to these foreign pieces with sudden and violent storms of misfiring neurons around the damaged area. It was epilepsy at its worst, with seizures striking him many times a day, every day. All kinds of treatments were tried, and finally, in a last-ditch effort to rid W.J. of these attacks, it was decided to cut the corpus callosum to keep these neuron storms from spreading. The idea was to limit them to one side of the brain. It was certainly what Hippocrates would have called a desperate remedy for a desperate disease, but it worked. The operation was successful, and after several weeks, W.J. said he felt fine. Unlike Phineas Gage, his personality changed not at all.

It was after the surgery that W.J. met Dr. Roger Sperry and Dr. Michael Gazzaniga at the California Institute of Technology, where the cat experiments had taken place. The two doctors began a series of tests to see if, like the cats, there was any change in the way W.J. remembered things learned with one side or the other of the brain.

When W.J. was asked to raise his hand or bend his knee, he always raised his right hand or bent his right knee. It was as if his left brain could understand the words, but his right brain wasn't getting the message to lift the hand or knee under its control.

When W.J. was blindfolded and handed a comb, he could tell what it was. Still blindfolded with the same hand that had held the comb, he could reach into a box full of objects and pick out the comb. But if he was asked to reach into the box with the other hand, he could not pick out the comb.

If the word "comb" was flashed on the left side of a screen where only the right side of his brain got the message, W.J. could reach out with his left hand (run by his right brain) and pick out the comb lying among other objects. But he could not say the word comb. With the corpus callosum cut, there was no longer a bridge to carry messages from one side of the brain to the other.

To test split-brain patients, equipment similar to this was arranged so that when a word is flashed on the screen, only one hemisphere can see it. The patient tries to pick up the object he saw on the screen. Even though the patient reads the word with his left brain, his right brain does not get the message, and his left hand doesn't know which thing to pick up.

W.J. became a man whose right hand literally did not know what his left hand was doing. Sometimes his left hand would do something his right hand didn't like. He would try to pull down his trousers with one hand while the other hand tried to yank them up. If his left hand tried to sort a set of blocks or pile the blocks to match another stack, his right hand would reach out and destroy what his left hand had done.

It began to look as though W.J.'s left brain was the smart one, the one that could read and write and speak, while his right brain was the dumb one, the minor hemisphere.

Humans have always had a sense of the difference between their brain halves, especially the feeling that the right brain, and therefore the left hand, was not quite up to par with its other half. We speak of a left-handed compliment, which is not a compliment at all.

The right hand (and left brain) has been identified with goodness, and things that are honest, proper, or moral. We swear oaths with the right hand, salute with the right hand, and shake with the right hand. The left hand (with its supposedly weaker right brain) has never had this good context. In fact, the Latin word for left is *sinister*, meaning bad or ominous. The Latin for right is *dexter*, which is the base for the word "dexterity," meaning skillful.

The word "left" comes from the old Anglo-Saxon word *lyft*, which means weak or worthless, while the Anglo-Saxon word for right is *reht*, which means straight or just. It was only a few years ago that people stopped the practice of discouraging left-handed children from using their left hand. It was common in schools a hundred years ago to tie a child's left hand to force him to use his right. Left-handedness was considered awkward, clumsy, and somehow not quite right. Betty Edwards's book *Drawing on the Right Side of Your Brain* says, "Now, it's important to remember that these terms were all made up, when languages began, by some person's left hemispheres—the left brain called the right brain bad names! And the right brain—labeled, pinpointed, and buttonholed—was without a language of its own to defend itself."

At first, the research seemed to confirm the old idea of the right brain as the weaker side. But then, during one of the tests, W.J. was shown a diagram of a Greek cross and asked to copy it with his left hand. Although W.J. was right-handed, he picked up the pencil and quickly copied the cross with one smooth continuous line. When they asked him to copy it with his dominant right hand, he drew five or six unconnected lines that suggested about half of the design, and he said he was finished. His left brain was not getting messages about space and line relationships.

The right brain was not stupid after all. It was just doing different things. As data was collected from other split-brain patients, it became apparent that while the right brain may not be able to read and write, it can think and express emotions and draw. The right brain is better, in fact, at seeing the total picture, assessing a complete situation. It is better at any job requiring the person to recognize patterns, shapes, faces, or complicated objects.

A brilliant composer had a stroke affecting his left brain, so that he could not speak and could not write musical notes on paper. But his career was not over because he could still compose music, play it, and remember it.

The split-brain patients taught us a lot about our two cooperating hemispheres. There is a constant sharing of information between the two working halves, a stream of information across the corpus callosum tying together the separate talents and stored experiences of each half.

When a baby is born, its corpus callosum is not fully developed. Everything a baby sees, hears, and learns goes to both sides of the brain equally. The hemispheres develop as duplicates. By the time a child is two, one side or the other begins to dominate, and the communication between the two halves improves until age fifteen, when it levels off. Specialization begins early in life, and we are shaped by the world around us. Born with billions of neurons ready to make new connections as we learn, we also have a basic set of plans—the information of our species that is carried in our DNA.

There is a great deal of interest in the right brain lately, as though educating the right brain will solve the problems of schools. Like phrenology and alpha-wave training and biofeedback, right-left brain studies have become a fad. There is a push to include more "right-brain activities" in the schools, which some see as a danger because it is the more left-brained skills of reading and writing that are vital in our culture.

"The most common error in thinking about the hemispheres," says science writer Daniel Goleman, "is to attribute one or another mental activity strictly to the right half or left half . . . as if one switched on for, say, logic, and the other for spatial tasks."

A diagram in a news magazine showed the brain neatly divided down the middle, with language, math, and science on the left, and dance, art appreciation, and sculpture on the right. The truth is that during different mental tasks, one side of the brain is only *relatively* more active than the other. And for every mental process, many other parts of the brain are at work. None of the systems operates alone. When too much emphasis is placed on one part or one system, it distorts the picture of the whole brain.

Since the split-brain studies began, it has become apparent that the corpus callosum is more important than anyone suspected. When this bridge of nerve fibers malfunctions, it may be responsible for learning disabilities, one of which is called dyslexia. It is difficult for people with this disorder to read because words look backwards, or letters are mixed up. A *p* might look like a *q*, or a *b* like a *d*. This nerve-bridge might also be at fault in mental diseases so that reality and dreams get mixed up.

Right-left brain research may help us understand and encourage creativity and inventiveness. It has led to experiments to teach stroke victims to communicate with symbols instead of the words they can no longer say. A person whose left brain is blocked cannot speak, but he can retrain the right brain to pick out plastic letters and symbols to spell out words.

Albert Einstein, a brilliant mathematician and physicist, described himself as a visual person. In other words, he was right-brained. He had to "see" three-dimensional images in his mind before he could write the equations. He had a terrible time in school. One teacher expelled him because he was stupid and disrupted the class. He spent most of his time dreaming and imagining. He hated reading and traditional math and science. He wondered, as he got older, how many students lost the excitement of learning because they did not conform to the usual school methods. Perhaps the split-brain studies will make us more aware that both halves of the brain are equally valuable. Standard IQ tests favor the person with the left-brain verbal skills, but a person who excels at reading and writing is not necessarily brighter or better than someone who can paint or create a design or build a model. We ought to be more flexible. Most of us get in the habit of using one style of thinking, of expressing ourselves in the left-brain method of words, or staying with our right-brain actions. These studies should help us teach children to develop both sides, to learn to activate one side or the other consciously.

With electrodes on their heads, people have been given dull textbooks to read, and the brain activity is seen coming mostly from the left hemisphere, the verbal side. But when those same people are given exciting fiction, stories with action, colorful characters, and imagery, the right brain becomes much more active and both sides work together. Maybe if a history textbook, for example, was exciting, full of description and action, both sides of the brain would take notice and we'd learn faster. At least we'd be more attentive.

As the romance of the right-brain studies fades, we will return to the idea of a whole brain at work. As the brain is mapped and areas are assigned to functions, we still discover that all roads of the mental map still lead to the consciousness, the personality, the self. Right brain, left brain—both are important parts of a single, exceedingly complex system.

11 *Sweet Dreams and Jet Lag*

Some students work their way through college by sleeping. No special talent or experience is required. The employee arrives at one of the sleep labs in various research centers across the country, checks in, puts on his pajamas, and brushes his teeth. Before he goes to bed, he is fitted with a headful of electrodes, a blood pressure cuff, and other devices to monitor heart rate and temperature.

What can we find out from a sleeping person, and why do we want to know what happens during this time-out? We sleep away about one third of our lives, and that alone is reason for testing. Why do we sleep so much when some animals sleep not at all? Why do we dream, and why do we have problems when we're not allowed dream time?

The hours we lie unaware, close to but not quite unconscious, have intrigued man since his beginning. Every culture has created legends and myths to explain dreams and sleep. Now we explain them with scientific methods.

In the tombs of ancient Egyptian rulers, archeologists found wooden pillows carved in the image of Bes, the god of the highways. Bes was in charge of protecting the spirit of the sleeper on its night journey. It was the custom in many countries to wake a sleeper slowly, gently, so that his spirit had time to return to his body. It was unthinkable to startle a sleeper and leave his spirit stranded.

The habits and rituals of sleep are important. Everyone has some. Children want a special blanket, a particular worn, limp old teddy bear, or a comforting light left on. Adults need certain kinds of pillows, or just the right covers, or the windows closed or opened to an exact height. Charles Dickens went further than most in his sleep rituals: even when he traveled, staying at either city hotels or country inns, he rearranged the furniture, placing the bed so that he could sleep aligned with the magnetic fields, his head north and his feet south.

After the ritual of placing all the wires and apparatus on the volunteer at the sleep lab, the scientist tries to stay awake while the volunteer tries to sleep. During the night, the researcher watches the readout on all the equipment and wakes the volunteer at intervals to ask him what he is dreaming or to take blood samples.

The first sleep-for-science took place in the 1930s at the University of Chicago when Dr. Nathaniel Kleitman studied the sleep patterns of infants. He wasn't as interested in the babies' sleep as in the way their sleep patterns affected the adults kept awake. The unexpected turn in this research showed a pattern of sleep that repeated over and over in predictable cycles.

Research has determined the four stages of sleep. Stage one, when we are drifting off to sleep, lasts no more than five or six minutes. During this time the brain waves are large, slow alpha waves. When we move into stage two, the waves change to sharper spindles, and if a person is awakened during this time, he insists he has not been sleeping. In stage three the EEG begins to show great peaks and valleys on the graph. The heart rate slows, the blood pressure drops, and so does body temperature. This is what we'd call "sound asleep." Stage four shows an even greater tracing of the slow waves, and now it is even harder to wake the sleeper. In this stage the growth hormone is at work in children, and they literally grow while they're asleep. This fourth stage is the time of sleepwalking or -talking, of terrifying nightmares seldom remembered unless the sleeper wakes.

We are never unconscious during any of these stages. We

can be awakened by a touch, by the smell of smoke, the stab of pain, the sound of a mosquito. We change position many times, and the brain waves remain active, sometimes more active than when we are awake.

This activity was one of the surprises of sleep studies. When Hans Berger put his new EEG machine on sleeping volunteers, he fully expected the sleep patterns to show slow, large waves similar to those of total relaxation. But suddenly the sleeper's brain waves became active, the tracings jumping up and down as though the person were awake. Such action takes place on a cycle of more or less ninety minutes. It is called paradoxical sleep because it is such a contradiction, because strangely enough (paradoxically) there is more electrical activity then than when a person is awake. More commonly this stage is called REM sleep, named for the rapid eye movements back and forth during this stage as though the eyes are watching a movie screen. It is the time of dreaming, and everyone dreams, whether they remember or not.

Dreams, some say, allow us to stay sane, allow us to be safely and quietly insane for a little while each night, to clear out unwanted information and sort out information to be stored. About one fifth of a night's sleep plays host to dreams.

As this REM sleep begins, the heart rate quickens, the breathing becomes more rapid, and the blood pressure goes up. The brain waves quicken, although the person lies quite still. The blood supply to the brain increases, leaving the muscles with less tone, which keeps us from getting up to act out the dreams. Just before the dream begins, the sleeper shifts and changes position just like a person shifting in a theater seat before the movie starts.

All mammals dream. Newborn kittens, rats, and rabbits show only REM sleep, which makes one wonder what they dream about. Cats sleep away 60 to 70 percent of their lives. Human babies spend about half of their sleep in this REM stage. Is it a rehearsal time for them, a time when some ancestral memories are being written in the brain cells?

When the REM-sleep idea was proposed, many disagreed. If the theory was right, if eyes moved because they were "watching" the action of the dream-movie, then it should also be true that blind people would not have such movements because they do not see. When blind volunteers slept at the research lab, they went through the usual stages of sleep. During dream time their EEG waves matched those of sighted people, but their eyes did not move. Those who had been blind since birth dreamed in sound and smells, but those who had lost sight later in life held onto the memory of sight and dreamed with some eye movement.

When REM sleep is repeatedly interrupted, the sleeper makes up that REM time at the first opportunity, going into that stage much more quickly than usual. Lack of sleep will kill more quickly than lack of food. One of the best-known experiments on sleep deprivation was actually a publicity stunt. Peter Tripp was a disc jockey in New York who decided to stay awake for two hundred hours in a "wake-athon" for the March of Dimes. He had a physical exam before the event, and a doctor was there each day to check Tripp's blood, urine, brain waves, and heart. In addition, Tripp ate high-protein foods. The first three days nothing much happened, except that he had trouble keeping his eyes open.

On the fourth day Tripp began seeing things. He saw a rabbit in the booth with him, and specks on the table began to look like spiders. On the fifth day, although his general health was good, Tripp was having more severe and frequent hallucinations. He saw flames jumping from drawers and furry worms crawling on everything. He couldn't say the alphabet or remember recent events. Although he looked awake, his EEG readings changed to resemble those of someone asleep. When his grueling test was over, he was like a man insane, but as soon as he caught up on his sleep he was all right.

Hallucinations are an occupational hazard for truck drivers, radar scanners, or anyone facing long periods of monotony like straight stretches of road or a screen with regular patterns that seldom change. When the brain isn't getting enough sensory messages from the outside, it begins to listen to its own internal messages. It mixes dreams and reality, and during waking hours these dreams are called hallucinations. Both dreams and hallucinations are regulated by the same chemical, a neurotransmitter called serotonin. It is the stuff that makes a "dream dam" to hold back the visual images that would make it seem as though we lived in two worlds.

Serotonin is concentrated in an area of the brainstem called the raphe nuclei. This area comprises a group of cells that has long branches reaching out to target cells in many areas of the brain, especially the visual and emotion-packed limbic systems. When serotonin flows across the synaptic gaps, it acts like a dam to keep the target cells from firing. It is inhibitory. But when the serotonin level drops during REM sleep, the chemical blockade is lifted and these target cells fire, freeing the images of dreams.

LSD causes explosions of visual images and hallucinations because it is so much like serotonin. The chemical structures of LSD and serotonin are enough alike to allow LSD to lift the "dream dam" as though it were the brain's own chemical. The difference between real dreams and LSD hallucinations is that the LSD-tripper is awake and is receiving a mixture of messages, some from the world around him and some from his own brain. The brain doesn't know which part of the mixture of drug-distorted and normal images are the real ones. We are protected from this crazy view of the world during the waking hours by the damming of our dreams.

In recent years the sleeping-pill business has boomed, until now between two and three billion pills are taken in the United States each year. Unfortunately, they don't produce healthy sleep. They only deaden the entire nervous system, much like an anesthetic. The important dream time is missing, and if the taker mixes the pills with alcohol or other drugs, there is a high risk of brain damage, coma, or death.

The Food and Drug Administration is testing a common food substance for use as a sleeping pill. It is an amino acid called L-tryptophan. Along with its job as a protein-builder, it is used by the brain to make the dream-damming serotonin. Even one gram of this amino acid (which would be equal to the tryptophan in a large meal) allows a person to fall asleep faster. Because it is a substance found in meat and dairy products, it is expected that L-tryptophan will prove to be safe and certainly not habit-forming. It won't destroy the normal sleep patterns, and the taker can count on his ninety-minute cycle to go undisturbed. This chemical may well be the reason that a glass of warm milk or cocoa helps a person sleep.

During the sleep studies, it was found that we continue on this bio-cycle night and day. Although the time varies with individuals from seventy to 120 minutes, it averages ninety minutes, alternating between peaks and lows of mental activity. Tests show that artists and others who work in creative fields are more imaginative in this cycle, with ideas coming easier every forty-five minutes, followed by a low period forty-five minutes later. It accounts for that feeling every once in a while of not being able to concentrate, followed a while later by that "Aha, now I've got it" feeling. With a little luck, it might be possible to hit one of these mental peaks during math class or a gymnastics tournament and a low at lunch, although it seems to happen the other way around more often than not.

Thomas Edison is famous for the way he took advantage of this cycle, going to extremes. He would catnap every now and then, no matter where he was or who he was with. He could fall asleep easily and awake fifteen or twenty minutes later refreshed and ready to tackle a new idea.

This regular rhythm of life can be disturbed by travel. Nothing in our ancient past equipped us to handle jet lag. The brain's clock turns body temperature down at night and up during the day and regulates our hormones. Indeed, all our systems work by this inner clock. The brain's clock stays on its own time whether we turn our watches ahead or back for a new time zone, and that's the problem. Traveling from New York to Europe can leave a person feeling depressed, with no energy and no appetite. In a few days a holiday traveler adjusts, but it is a bigger problem for pilots and flight attendants to shift back and forth continuously. It is a problem for nurses and others who must alternate between night and day shifts.

As they look for chemicals to treat the jet-lag problem, scientists hope also to find the key to treating patients with severe mental depression because their symptoms are so similar to those of jet lag. They believe the brain's clock in these people may be off its timing.

The space program has studied sleep patterns as it monitored astronauts for long periods and discovered that, even on the moon, the astronauts kept to their inner brain time. No one is really sure how the neurons work to keep us on this cycle of roughly ninety minutes, or why they do. The answer will be found some day in the chemical and electrical interactions between and within these still-mysterious cells.

12 *Dr. Mesmer's Big Idea*

Get control of your life. Stop smoking. Lose weight. Study better. Remember more. Learn faster.

Hypnosis is often advertised as the answer to every problem. In groups or alone, people are being hypnotized to face the dentist's drill, to remember long-forgotten incidents, or to break old habits. The technique is not new. Under a variety of names it has been used in many cultures through the ages. It is not magic, but it is mysterious. No one knows how it works, only that it does work. Hypnosis is not a fake treatment, but there are those who fake it, sensationalize it, and make it seem more mystical and miraculous than it is.

Dr. Franz Mesmer has gone down in history as one of the greatest fakers of them all, although he is also called the father of hypnotism. One biographer, James Wycoff, called him "a discoverer whose discovery was denied in his own day." His "day" was the 1770s, the time of Galvani, Volta, and the new science of electricity. Mesmer studied theology to please his parents. Then he went to law school for a while and earned a doctorate in philosophy. Finally he went to medical school. He was thirty-one when he became a doctor, and the title of his thesis was "Concerning the

Influence of the Planets." Mesmer was a man of many interests, especially astrology and the cosmic forces. He believed in a life force, a kind of universal energy he called the fluidium, and he combined this with his interest in magnets and the much discussed "animal electricity."

He found that some of his patients were cured of pains when he passed magnets over their bodies. As he experimented more, he found that he could produce these same cures without the magnets. Just the "passing of hands" over the patient would do it. He called it animal magnetism; others called it mesmerism.

The doctors in Vienna did not take kindly to this new method, and Mesmer was charged with malpractice. The laying-on-of-hands was not new, but Mesmer seemed to be carrying it too far. The royal touch was an old custom of early monarchs, who healed the commoners of the king's evil by touching them. The "evil" is

Dr. Mesmer's treatments became popular as social events. This old engraving shows a drawing-room scene in which patients hold iron rods in the wooden tub in order to receive the magnetism that was part of the treatment. (NATIONAL LIBRARY OF MEDICINE)

reported to have been some swelling of the neck, perhaps goiters, and some say it was epilepsy. Louis XIV touched sixteen hundred people one spectacular Easter Sunday.

When Mesmer moved his practice to Paris, his cures became the rage, a fad, almost a cult. He attracted the wealthy and famous, including the Mozart family, to his salons where he "cured" in splendor. The darkened room was lavishly decorated with thick carpets and heavy draperies. Soft music played in the background. In the center of the room stood a *baquet,* an oak tub five feet in diameter, much like the hot tubs sold today. The patients sat around the outside of the tub and held onto bent iron rods that stuck out of the lid. Mesmer's tub was lined with layers of bottles full of "magnetized" water. Some of the patients fainted, screamed, and even convulsed as they claimed to feel the magnetism enter their bodies. It was a dramatic way to go to the doctor, and it wasn't long before the doctors of Paris formed a commission to investigate. It consisted of such experts in magnetism and electricity as Benjamin Franklin (who had recently flown his kite), Lavoisier (the brilliant chemist who was to lose his head in the guillotine), and Joseph Guillotin (who invented the deadly device). Mesmer was asked to leave Paris. He died in 1815, virtually unknown, but others continued his work. Most agree that Mesmer probably did cure some ailments by suggestion alone.

In 1841, a Scottish surgeon, James Braid, saw a demonstration of Mesmerism, and he began to experiment on his patients. He found that he could induce a trancelike state in which a person was unusually open to suggestion. He described it not as magnetism, but as a suspension of the conscious mind, a mind weary from repetition. He called this state of mind hypnotic and the technique hypnotism, taking the name from the Greek word for sleep.

Others used the technique, including an English surgeon, Dr. John Elliotson, who operated with the aid of a trancelike state, but he was dismissed from his post at London University for practicing those "sickly French theories." They remembered Mesmer. When Sigmund Freud used hypnotism as part of his treatment, it gave the method some professional status, but others turned it into show business, a carnival side-show attraction. Hypnotism still has two sides. It is a reputable medical treatment, and it is still a popular night-club and television act.

Ordinarily we are limited by what we believe we can and

cannot do. Hypnosis helps us give up our doubts. We believe what the hypnotist tells us we can do.

Four steps lead to the hypnotic states: suggestion, visualization, focus, and suspension of judgment. First, the hypnotist suggests that you can do something—stop smoking, lose weight, feel numb in your arm, whatever. Then he helps you visualize yourself not smoking, or thin, or numb. Next, he helps you focus on that image, blocking out all other thoughts. The suspension of judgment means you will no longer judge whether you can or cannot, will or will not do this selected thing. Instead, you go ahead as if you can. The as-if action is an important one.

When the French Academy of Science was investigating Dr. Mesmer, one of the accusations was that his patients were cured by vivid imaginations. One of the scientists on the panel is reported to have said that if it was so, what a marvelous thing imagination must be.

Hypnosis is imagining and believing that you can feel no pain, remember a long-forgotten event, or break an old habit. One doctor who uses it regularly in his practice describes hypnosis as a pupil-teacher relationship. The hypnotic state can be achieved alone, but it is easier with a teacher-hypnotist to direct you, to provide information and discipline.

Nobody knows what chemical changes take place in the brain during hypnosis, or whether there are any changes. It is not easy to examine the brain of a hypnotized rat, much less that of a hypnotized person. So it remains a technique unexplained. Animals can be mesmerized, however. At alligator farms one of the popular demonstrations is mesmerizing a big reptile by flipping it on its back and rubbing its stomach slowly until it goes limp.

Circumstances can hypnotize. A driver traveling a long, dull stretch of road with nothing to distract him will suddenly be jolted out of his weary-mind state by a sound of an approaching car. A person can be so intent, concentrating on a picture, listening to music, staring at the ocean, as to be unaware of anything else. This kind of concentration makes it possible to induce a trancelike state that will allow a person to have major surgery without anesthetic.

Experts disagree on whether or not hypnosis is dangerous and whether a person can be hypnotized against his will. It can be dangerous if done by a disreputable or unethical person with intent to harm. Certainly no one can be deeply hypnotized for surgery if he doesn't want to be. But a person who says, "I'll bet you can't hypnotize me," might just be a challenge to a good hypnotist who can find the right focus, the right suggestions to make that person suspend judgment and act "as if" in a carefully selected situation.

Hypnotism requires complete attention, and it is impossible to hypnotize a person who is drunk, high on drugs, severely mentally retarded, or schizophrenic. Some people expect that hypnotism will miraculously solve problems. Seven women interviewed a few weeks after being hypnotized to lose weight reported an immediate *gain* in weight. Their expectations did not include the fact that they would still have to work at losing weight. Apparently they did expect calories to have no effect. The hypnotist explained that the suggestion, the focus, was made to help a conscious choice, to shore up will power, not to substitute for it.

Hypnotism is not a cure-all, but it is highly effective in many areas. Dentists use it to eliminate the gagging reflex when they have to fit dentures or make impressions for braces. They use it to slow the flow of saliva or to control bleeding. It can be used to change the patient's perception of time so that hours of wearing an uncomfortable retainer or new dentures can seem like minutes.

At Roswell Park Memorial Institute, a cancer-research hospital in Buffalo, New York, hypnotism has been used for years to help patients adjust to artificial limbs. People who have lost an arm or leg sometimes experience pain, which can be eliminated by hypnotism, in the "phantom limb." When drugs no longer control the pain of cancer, sometimes hypnotism can.

Women have delivered babies by the surgical technique called a Caesarian section with no anesthetic other than hypnosis. Many other women have been hypnotized to feel no pain from the waist down when delivering a baby in the normal way. Medical schools include hypnosis training as a technique to use whenever it can supplement regular treatments or replace difficult or painful treatments.

Police departments occasionally employ hypnotists to help witnesses recall details of crimes and to locate missing persons. Psychiatrists use hypnosis to help patients remember past events that might explain fears or feelings.

There are few scientific facts about hypnosis. It does not work in every case or on every person, but when it does work, it is an amazing phenomenon of mind over matter.

13 *The Mind Changers*

The arena was silent. There were no cheers, no shouting. One man walked to the center of the ring, but he carried no cape, only a tiny black box. He signaled, and from across the arena a door swung open. A brave bull pawed the ground, lowered his head, and charged. The man stood confident and still. As the bull pounded across the ring to within a few feet of his target, the man pressed a button on the black box. The bull skidded to a stop and dropped to the ground. The bull was fully conscious, but he was no longer in control of his muscles. Dr. José Delgado had stopped him with a radio-transmitted signal to an electrode in the bull's brain.

The charging bull was an overly dramatic demonstration of Dr. Delgado's experiments in brain control. Many of his critics accuse Delgado of show-off tactics, and compared with the usual rat-running experiments in most laboratories, it is fair criticism.

Delgado and his team at Yale University planted electrodes in the brains of rats, cats, monkeys, and a chimp named Paddy during the 1960s. Early attempts at wiring the brains of animals for outside control had one major problem: they weren't monkey-proof. Wires coming from the heads of cats and rats were no more bothersome to the animals than leashes, but the monkeys were ingenious at damaging the wires and sometimes hurting themselves. It was understandable. It was not the most pleasant thing in the world to wear wires on the head. But Delgado found that he could eliminate this problem by using radio-controlled devices, without wires.

Electrodes in Paddy's brain communicated to a two-way radio and through that to a computer. The computer could detect the brain patterns associated with different moods and actions of the chimp. Whenever Paddy's patterns showed that he was getting aggressive or boisterous, the radio sent signals to the electrodes buried in the almond-shaped amygdala deep in Paddy's brain, as well as to electrodes in his brain stem. This produced a very unpleasant sensation, and it didn't take long for Paddy to learn how to turn off those feelings. All he had to do was become a quiet, docile animal instead of an aggressive one. When the computer controls stopped, it took about two weeks for Paddy to return to his normal behavior.

Dozens of experiments were done in which contented cats became vicious attackers. Or a cat could be made to drop a mouse it had just killed and was about to eat. Monkeys became aggressors or underdogs, depending on where the stimulation was received. Rats learned to press buttons that stimulated the pleasure center of the brain, doing so until they dropped from exhaustion.

Such experiments revealed the functions of inner parts of the brain as Penfield's probes had mapped the surface of the cortex. Delgado became outspoken in his campaign to use electrical stimulation for control. Hot arguments raged about the ethics of such use, especially on patients with histories of violent behavior. Followers of Delgado recommended the technique for use on prisoners who could not be otherwise controlled, and even on children labeled aggressive in schools.

"I am not so naïve as to think that cerebral research holds all the answers to mankind's present problems, but . . ." Delgado has said. His *but* led other scientists to say that Delgado's hopes are other people's fears. The question is, where does it stop? Who will be the judge of the kind of behavior that needs to be controlled by electrodes?

Like all research, it has its good and bad uses. The technique's good side has been seen in the control of involuntary motions like the tremors of Parkinson's disease. It has also been used to control pain that no longer responds to drugs.

In England, G. S. Brindley and W. Levin have implanted electrodes in the visual cortex of blind patients. By stimulating combinations of electrodes, they can transmit patterns like those of Braille letters, which patients can read faster than with their fingertips. It is an expensive technique, still in the experimental stage, but it is a step towards doing for the blind what hearing aids do for the deaf.

Long before the idea of implanting electrodes in the brain, there was a technique for controlling violence so simple that it could be done with an ice pick. Just as Phineas Gage's hole in the head changed his personality from even-tempered to aggressive, so surgeons found they could change violent mental patients into docile ones. It started with some frustrated chimpanzees.

The first psychosurgical operations were done on a group of chimpanzees who lived in a research lab where they were given problems to solve to find out how quickly they learned. When they couldn't solve the problems easily, the chimps screamed and rattled their cages and had tantrums. One of the scientists thought that if he took out the frontal lobes of the chimps, it might change their personalities, and it did. When the animals recovered from surgery they were amiable, cooperative, friendly chimps, and they went back to their problem-solving tasks. They made more mistakes after the operation, but they didn't seem to care; no more tantrums, no more terrorizing the other chimps.

In 1935, Dr. Antonio Caetano de Abreu Freire Egas Moniz, a surgeon from Portugal, attended a conference where he heard the story of the tranquilized chimps. Moniz was well known for a process he introduced called an angiogram. It was a method of injecting the blood vessels of the brain so they could be seen by x-ray. When he heard about the chimps, he thought this technique might help some of his patients who were in mental hospitals with uncontrollable fits of violence and temper.

Moniz found that he did not need to cut out the entire forebrain. He had only to probe it with a long needle and cut the nerve fibers leading to the inner brain. The results were dramatic. Patients who at one time had to be restrained in strait jackets or placed in padded cells now were calm. However, there was a price to pay. The calm patients were also dull. They sort of shuffled through life with no sense of responsibility, no ambition, no initiative or creativity. There were a few notable exceptions, persons who were able to return to normal lives, but it is thought that in those cases the nerve fibers were not completely cut or the brain compensated somehow by using other areas for similar functions.

At any rate, lobotomies, as the operations were called, became a common mental treatment. In the 1940s, thousands of patients were lobotomized, including alcoholics, who continued to drink but no longer cared. By 1954, there were fifty thousand recorded lobotomies in the United States, but the operation was banned in Russia in 1950. Dr. Moniz was awarded a Nobel Prize in 1949 for this new technique of psychosurgery.

The lobotomies were undoubtedly better than early treatments in which people were put in mental hospitals and chained, beaten, and often ignored. But it still wasn't the answer. Suddenly

One of the most humane treatments for people in the old "insane asylums" was this tranquilizing chair, which was intended to calm patients.
(NATIONAL LIBRARY OF MEDICINE)

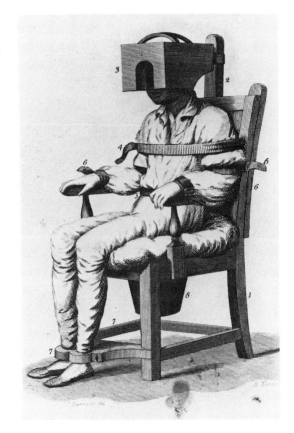

in 1952, the number of lobotomies dropped drastically because the first psychoactive drugs were on the market, drugs that produced the same effect without the cost or the permanent damage of lobotomies.

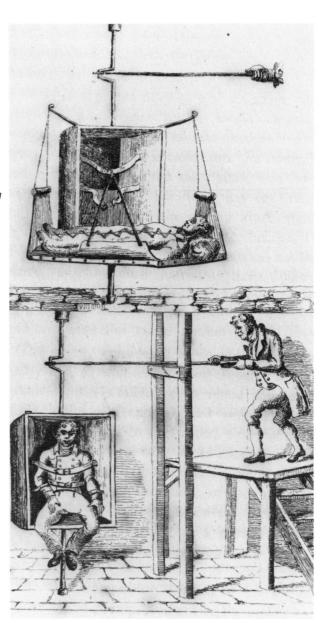

Benjamin Rush's circulating swing was used to treat mental patients, perhaps on the theory that making them dizzy might in some way calm them or "sort out" their mixed-up minds.
(NATIONAL LIBRARY OF MEDICINE)

There were a lot of "old" drugs—caffeine, tobacco, alcohol, LSD, marijuana, sleeping pills, cocaine, morphine, heroin, amphetamines. But in 1952, some French scientists found a drug that literally changed the treatment of mental illness. While doing research on the antihistamines, which are used to control allergies like hay fever, they found the compound they called chlorpromazine. Although it wasn't until the 1970s that scientists discovered *how* it worked, chlorpromazine seemed like a miracle. It could turn agitated schizophrenic patients into calm, approachable people, and it had the same effect on some other disorders as well. It closed a dark era of medicine, years of misunderstanding and helplessness which frequently led to cruel treatment. It opened the door for the effective use of occupational therapy, group-therapy discussions, and other treatments that are almost useless if the patient is uncontrollable.

Drugs are as old as man. There has always been some kind of plant that could produce a cure, a happy feeling, or some mind change. Each step of civilization seems to have added yet another drug, and there are no sharp lines between the ones that are useful and the ones that are harmful. Often they are the same drug.

In 1808, Friedrich Serturner, a chemist's assistant, isolated the most active substance in opium. He produced a white powder he called "morphium," named after the Roman god of sleep, Morpheus. Opium, used in many ancient cultures for pleasure as well as treatment of disease, is unpredictable because, when mixed with other substances or when the dosage is high, it kills the patient instead of the pain. Morphine was a purer substance, although it turned out to be more addictive.

Laboratories everywhere tried to find drugs that were not addictive. In 1898 some chemists at a Bavarian dye-works thought they had found one. Working with the morphine molecule, they found a pain-killing drug almost eight times as powerful as morphine with no indications that it was addictive. So happy were they with their heroic efforts that they called the new drug heroin. Of course, heroin turned out to be even more addictive than its parent, morphine.

Cocaine, which had been used for centuries in folk medicine, was isolated as a drug in 1860. South American Indians chewed the coca leaves to get the effects of cocaine, but no one took much notice of the new drug until the 1880s when Sigmund Freud began to use it. He tried to help morphine addicts break their habit by substituting cocaine. He was so enthusiastic about the drug that he called it a "divine plant" that "strengthens the weak and makes them forget their misfortune." He told others of the self-control, the exhilaration, the joy that could be theirs with cocaine. He sent some to his fiancée, his sisters, and friends. Sniffing cocaine became the social fad of the 1880s. It had a second wave of popularity during World War I, and by the 1920s its evils were well known as people died from overdoses or experienced hallucinations that ended sometimes in complete insanity.

On it went. Barbiturates, amphetamines, tranquilizers, all became as common as aspirin is now. LSD was discovered in 1938, but it wasn't widely used until the 1960s. Albert Hoffmann worked for a drug company in Basel, Switzerland. He made a substance called lysergic acid diethylamide, shortened to LSD. He didn't remember how he did it, whether he accidentally got some of this new substance on a finger and then put that near his mouth, but he ingested some LSD. He reported feeling restless, dizzy, and ill, so he went home. The next day he felt fine and returned to work. The following week Hoffmann deliberately took a quarter of a milligram of LSD to find out if that had been the cause of his previous illness. A quarter milligram is a substantial dose, and he went on a six-hour "trip." When he started to feel sick, he asked his lab assistant to help him get home. They rode the four miles on bicycles because it was wartime and no cars were available. This time he experienced a full range of visual distortions, faces appearing as grotesque colored masks, and constantly changing colors. Sounds seemed transposed into visual sensations, and he shouted or babbled incoherent words. LSD is one of the most potent of drugs. The amount equal in size to an aspirin tablet would be enough to affect three thousand people. In the 1940s the United States Army tested LSD to assist in brainwashing and in making prisoners talk freely.

LSD became a useful drug in psychotherapy in mental institutions. It was quickly discovered that the kind of "trip" LSD produced depended greatly on the state of mind of the patient, so that a severely depressed, unstable person was likely to have a terrifying, nightmarish experience. Therapists learned to prepare the patient ahead of time, providing a relaxed atmosphere and guiding the person through a pleasant session that did seem to help shorten therapy time. LSD is now used to help terminally ill cancer patients cope with both the pain and stress. But anyone using the powerful drug without medical assistance runs the risk of finding his mind changed more than he may have wanted. LSD is one of the most dangerous drugs in existence. Many people have "tripped out" on it and never come back.

Drugs, of course, are useful, and it's hard to imagine some medical treatments without them. But drugs can also create enormous new problems, many of them worse than the problems they were used to solve in the first place. The "drug scene" is not limited to the young, nor is it the exclusive territory of the bored middle-aged person or the overworked executive popping tranquilizers or diet pills. Actually, drugs are more a part of the life style of the elderly than of any other population group. The elderly comprise only 11 percent of the population, but they take 25 percent of the drugs. The grandparent generation doesn't hang around street corners or meet in bars looking for drugs, and most of their drugs are used to relieve aches and pains rather than to alter their minds. But even the legitimately prescribed drugs change minds in unpleasant ways when mixed with alcohol or other medications.

Sometimes the elderly save old drugs, then use them up without knowing whether the drugs have lost their potency or have changed chemically. Older people are often put on antidepressant drugs when their only problem may be loneliness. They become addicted to tranquilizers prescribed to make them less anxious when they may really be worried about having enough money to live on. There is no sharp line between good and bad use of drugs because the result always depends on why and how and when the drugs are used. Even aspirin can be dangerous.

It is not necessary to resort to electrodes or drugs to control people. The fact is that any leader can control minds without these expensive or difficult techniques. Hitler did it when he controlled a nation through persuasive speeches and unrelenting propaganda and fear. It is done daily on television as we watch the hypnotically repeated ads that convince us to buy what we do not need or even want.

The term "brainwashing" was born during the 1950s when prisoners taken by Communist forces during the Korean War signed confessions and cooperated with the enemy. Called traitors by American newspapers, these war prisoners were victims of a method they did not know how to fight because it worked against the very nature of the mind. It was called "depersonalizing and re-education."

The brainwashers had learned that a brain deprived of activity will soak up any kind of information or stimulation to escape the boredom. Prisoners never knew what would happen next, so they were always in a state of anxiety and stress. They were kept in solitary confinement, isolated from everyone but a guard, on whom they came to depend. The cell was constantly lighted or completely dark for days. Sleep was interrupted after a few minutes rest, or the prisoner was not allowed to sleep at all. They were humiliated in front of others or threatened with immediate death, only to find a few days later the offer of kindness and sympathy. The terrible monotony and boredom, the total lack of any sound, of anything to look at but cell walls, of any kind of sensory stimulation, made the prisoners relieved—even happy—to listen to propaganda they would otherwise know was untrue.

They are the same techniques used by cults to make their members totally dependent. Young people who are wondering what direction their lives should take, who have no commitments, are easy prey to the open, friendly advances of cult members. Once interested, new members soon find themselves in what one ex-member described to Flo Conway and Jim Siegelman, authors of *Snapping,* as a "waking nightmare, a world devoid of free will."

Long periods with no sleep, no chance to make decisions or to act without permission, boring routines with little mental stimulation, humiliation in front of others—all make the person ready to accept the substitute stimulation of the cult's beliefs. Most of the cults are described as "intense experiences which affect the fundamental information-processing capacities of the brain," experiences that go much deeper than mere belief. They become real personality changes.

History's most horrifying example of a cult's power was made known on November 18, 1978, when nine hundred people committed suicide in Jonestown, Guyana. Men, women, and children lined up and drank poisoned Kool-Aid, urged on by their hypnotic, persuasive leader, Jim Jones, who had built his own church, his own society. Jonestown was described as a cloistered, no-escape world, with Jones the master of deception. He used a sophisticated recruiting system that preyed upon lonely, impressionable people. He weakened family ties, breaking husband-and-wife relationships. He used all the brainwashing methods of threat, humiliation, no sleep, poor nutrition, isolation, boredom. The few who escaped have called it a "frightful emotional experience that went far beyond the mass contagion of most evangelistic services."

In the 1970s people were jailed for kidnaping their own children from such cults as the Hare Krishna, Scientology, and the Moonies (Unification Church) in order to have them "deprogramed." A man named Ted Patrick is called "Black Lightning" by cult members because he was the first to point out the dangers of cults and try to get people out of them. He has been jailed and released several times, but those who have been successfully deprogramed praise his efforts.

Patrick believes that by "artful and deceiving means" the cults are robbing people of their natural capacity to think. He claims the cults use fear, guilt, hate, fatigue, and poor diet, and his defense in court is based on freedom of thought. The cults defend themselves on the grounds of freedom of speech and religion. It is difficult to define the line between a cult and a legitimate religion.

In *Snapping*, Flo Conway and Jim Siegelman describe a common experience of cult members. Almost always there is a moment recalled by members as "snapping," a time when the mind clicked into place as though weary from the repetition and deprivation, a time when it seemed to say, "Okay, okay, I believe you."

All of learning is brainwashing to some degree. One scientist has said that the brain was born to learn. We can't help learning; it's what we are made to do. A baby's brain begins to enrich its connections of neurons as soon as it is born, and it doesn't stop until death. We may each be born with a different capacity to learn, but almost certainly few of us use our brains to the fullest extent.

In one laboratory a group of rats were put in a playroom full of toys, an enormous cage filled with tunnels to explore, ledges to climb, holes to hide in. It was an "enriched" environment compared with that of their cousins, who stayed in small, uninteresting, ordinary lab cages. After eighty days the brains of the rats were examined, and the "playroom" rats' brains were bigger. Not only was the cortex thicker, but the cell bodies of neurons were larger and the number of glial cells greater. Certain enzymes and neurotransmitters were more abundant in the "enriched" rats. Other groups of rats spent only two hours a day for thirty days in this playroom, which produced the same results.

These "enriched" rats were not as "bright" as young rats living in the wild, rats who had to find their own food and keep away from enemies, but they were definitely better off than their dull-cage cousins.

Children raised in poverty areas, with not enough to eat, nowhere to play, and nothing to read or no one to read to them do not have as good a chance in school as children in an enriched atmosphere. Of course, children's brains can't be weighed and measured, but there are all kinds of ways to find out who is learning faster and better. It has been possible to raise the IQs of such poverty students by as much as twenty points when they get a chance to work and play in a stimulating environment.

There is an ancient Oriental saying, "I hear and I forget; I see and I remember; I do and I understand." Even without batteries of tests, we know that when we do something for ourselves, we do not forget. When we have to figure out a problem, we learn it better and remember it longer than if someone tells us the answer. The *doing* seems to help place the facts into the holographic memory system, filing it away as a greater variety of sensory clues from which we can select.

"Do your own thing" is not bad advice when it comes to building your brain power, and changing your own mind.

14 *What Happens Next?*

Even if the fictional Dr. Prentice could talk to his experimental, disembodied brain, he might never find out exactly how it works. Brain research, for all the millions of dollars spent on it, for all the scientists devoting careers to it, may never answer the age-old question of mind versus brain. Who is the ghost in the machine?

Even when all the neurotransmitters are identified, it will be like knowing all the letters of the alphabet but being a long way from knowing how to put them together to read Shakespeare. Brain research can't be put into one neatly packaged category. As the organ that controls all the other organs of the body, the brain is a territory that has to be explored by all the branches of science. The latest to enter the field are physics and mathematics.

Physics uses a method called quantum mechanics. The particles in atoms behave like waves, and the calculations of these wave functions are figured by quantum mechanics, calculations that can show how chemicals react and what their products will be like. Predictions can be made about the way the molecules will group under different conditions. The trouble used to be that these equations were much too complicated for practical use in chemistry. The problems were just too hard to solve. But now, with computers, precise answers about bondings between atoms are possible.

Among other things, using quantum mechanics in the search for neurotransmitters may make it unnecessary to experiment on animals or humans. The use of quantum mechanics may make it possible to predict which key will fit which lock without actually constructing experimental locks and keys. New drugs and medicines can be made without long series of tests. A chemist will be able to draw a blueprint of molecules just as an engineer draws a blueprint of the girders that make up a bridge. A drug can be "built" from a blueprint. Dr. Joyce Kaufman, who heads the team at Johns Hopkins doing this work with neurotransmitters, believes that it will be possible to predict if a chemical will cause cancer. When an industry produces a new product, whether a drug or a heating fuel, scientists can know in the building stage if the waste products can be safely buried or put into rivers. This blending of physics, chemistry, mathematics, biology, and computer science makes possible discoveries never dreamed of by Galvani, Golgi, or Galen.

Dr. Jerre Levy, who was part of the team that worked on the first split-brain studies, is discovering differences between the male and female brain. It will be a hotly debated issue before all the facts are in, and Dr. Levy hastens to remind us that it has nothing whatever to do with the equality of men and women as citizens. It has to do with the organization of the brain, and it may affect the way we educate children in the future.

We have thought for a long while that the sex differences in learning and skills are cultural—that is, stemming from our early training. Girls are given dolls to play with; boys are given trucks. Dr. Levy points out that men are better at maps and mazes and mathematics, while women seem to excel in verbal skills. Women's intuition seems to be a fact rather than an old wives' tale. It does not for one minute mean that women cannot continue to be excellent engineers or architects any more than it means men cannot continue to be excellent chefs, writers, or tailors. Dr. Levy's early findings describe how the hormone differences influence the organization of the brain. It is partly a matter of genetic inheritance, a part of ancient memory of skills learned and performed for millions of years, and partly the influence of biological functions.

Research on the sex differences in the brain is barely out of the first stages of planning. How should it be tested? What statistics should be collected? There is much to learn.

Spin-offs of all kinds come out of the basic research on the brain. Manufacturers are paying ad agencies to find out which commercials on television are most effective. Several new companies now use a simplified EEG machine to find out the interest level of TV viewers. People are hooked up to the machine with electrodes on their heads. As they watch commercials and programs, the EEG machine records the activity of waves in the right and left halves of the brain. It indicates when a mind is wandering and when it is attentive. If the right brain shows more activity, the person is responding to what he sees, but if the left brain shows greater waves, he is paying more attention to the message. The agencies evaluate whether commercials evoke "positive interest," but, of course, the tests don't really show whether interest is positive or negative. "You can be equally interested in Adolf Hitler or Winston Churchill," says an agency person. "You may hate one and love the other, but your level of interest may be the same."

Brain research goes in many directions. Some labs are looking for causes and cures to epilepsy, strokes, tumors, multiple sclerosis, dyslexia, and senility.

Some scientists think that the forgetting and confusion called senility may be caused by a slow virus. Kuru was a mysterious illness among a New Guinea tribe called the Fore. Victims trembled and shivered in a horrible kind of death-dance that lasted a year or more. Dr. Daniel Gajdusek, from the National Institute of Neurological Disorders, went to New Guinea and he saw a cannibalistic ritual in which women and children removed the brain tissue of the dead family member, squeezed it into a pulp, steamed it, and ate it. Without washing their hands afterwards, they would scratch, or wipe noses or eyes, and they virtually inoculated themselves with the virus-contaminated tissues. Kuru was a virus that spread quickly from person to person, but it did not appear until years later. The victim's brain showed signs of spongelike changes. Some of the things learned from kuru are being applied to the slow viruses that may be a part of multiple sclerosis and senility. It may be that a virus invades the brain and works slowly for several years, gradually causing the confusion of old age.

Brain surgery dates back to the Stone Age. Digging in ancient burial grounds, anthropologists found skulls that had been trepanned—that is, they had been drilled or cut open. The easiest explanation was that these were primitive people who believed in evil spirits and drilled holes in skulls to let out the demons, perhaps to cure unbearable headaches or madness. But when more than ten thousand such skulls taken from sites in Peru were studied carefully, it became apparent that surgeons had tried to remove shattered bits of bone that pressed against the brain. In one study of 400 trepanned skulls, there were 250 certain recoveries. (A recovery is recognized because bone has grown inwards to cover and heal the hole in the skull.)

In 1962, a Peruvian brain surgeon, Dr. Francesco Grana, performed surgery on a thirty-one-year-old patient under anesthetic, in a modern operating room, but instead of the usual surgical instruments, he used ancient (but sterilized) trepanning tools taken from burial sites. He was able to cut a hole in the patient's skull successfully and remove pressure from the brain. What today's surgeons have not figured out is how surgery was performed without anesthetics and with nothing to fight infection. How did they sew the flap of skin? How did they treat shock and stop the loss of blood? Perhaps they used a kind of hypnosis and drugs from the forests.

It wasn't until the mid-1800s that surgeons had anesthetics and antiseptics that allowed them to open the skull and expose the brain to operate for tumors. It has always been a risky operation. There was no way to pinpoint the tumor or to keep from damaging other brain tissue. But that has changed. Today a tumor can be precisely located with the CT scanner, and the surgeon can vaporize the tumor with a carbon-dioxide laser that touches no other tissue.

The tremors and shakes caused by diseases such as one called Parkinson's can be stopped by an electrode implanted with perfect accuracy at a site determined by microelectrode recordings. A patient can control his pain for up to twelve hours with a receiving coil placed under his collarbone and electrodes in his brain. An antenna is placed over the skin and current stimulates the electrode.

The boundaries of brain research seem endless. The more that basic research finds, the more applied research creates in the way of useful equipment and treatments that make life better. There is no single book that can describe everything that is known or is being investigated in the brain.

In October, 1980, the unexpected happened. The first brain transplant was done at the University of Rochester Medical School. It was not a complete brain transferred from one body to another. A piece of brain was removed from a rat with diabetes and replaced with a piece of brain from a healthy infant rat. The new section of brain survived and symptoms of the diabetes in the rat were gone. It is in no way even close to brain transplants for humans, but it is the first, all-important step.

Nobel Prize–winner Dr. Julius Axelrod pioneered work on the neurotransmitters. In an interview in *People* magazine, he said, "The study of the chemistry of the brain has a great future. We only need enough time, money, and bright young people to do the work."

The magnificent mind machine, the only machine that wonders about itself, is still the greatest frontier of science. Three pounds of tissue still holds more secrets than anything in this universe.

Acknowledgments

The complex subject of the human brain cannot, of course, be covered in a single book. We have tried to show the history of brain research, the state of research today, and the exciting possibilities of future investigations.

Many people have helped us, and we wish to thank them all, most especially Dr. John Warfel, State University of New York at Buffalo Medical School, who criticized the manuscript for us; Dr. Donald Donovan, East Aurora, New York, who talked to us at length about hypnosis; Dr. Philip Ament, who uses hypnosis in his dental practice and teaches it to medical and dental students; Dr. Reinhold Schlagenhauf, Erie County Medical Center, who allowed us to observe and talked to us about electroencephalography; Dr. Lee Bernardis, Veterans Hospital, Buffalo, New York, who showed us his neurological research project and checked our facts about neurons; Patricia Ulrich, who found the information for us about drugs; Donna Border, who suggested sources for us to investigate; the enthusiastic librarians at the Buffalo and Erie County Public Library; and our oldest son, Dr. Thomas Facklam, Battelle Institute, Columbus, Ohio, who suggested the subject in the first place; our youngest son, Paul, who did the jacket painting and the text illustrations; and our other children, David, John, and Peggy, who are always encouraging when we get involved in writing a book together and understand that now it's our turn to have the dining room table filled with books and papers.

Glossary

ALPHA WAVES. The long, slow brain waves of relaxation and inattention.

AMINO ACIDS. The basic building blocks of proteins. Proteins are composed of long chains of amino-acid molecules.

ANTHROPOLOGY. The science of man's physical and cultural origins.

AXON. A nerve fiber that carries impulses away from the cell body.

BETA WAVES. The fast, short brain waves of mental activity.

CENTRIFUGE. A device that rotates at high speed and separates substances of different densities.

CEREBELLUM. A part of the hindbrain that controls balance and coordinates the voluntary muscle movements.

CEREBRUM. The largest part of the brain in man. It controls voluntary muscles, perceives sensory input, and is responsible for original thought and memory.

COMPOUND MICROSCOPE. A microscope that has two lenses, an ocular lens and an objective lens.

CORPUS CALLOSUM. A large group of nerve fibers that connects the two halves of the cerebrum in mammals.

DENDRITE. A nerve fiber, usually branched, that carries impulses to the cell body.

DIABETES. The lack of the ability to control the amount of sugar in the blood.

DYSLEXIA. The impairment in the ability to read because of some brain defect.

ELECTROENCEPHALOGRAM (EEG). A record of the electrical activity of the brain.

EPILEPSY. A disorder of the nervous system usually characterized by seizures or convulsions.

ESB. Electrostimulation of the brain, or the process of stimulating certain areas of the brain with electrodes.

GALVANOMETER. A device that measures very small electrical currents.

GANGLIA. A mass of nerve cells that serve as relay centers.

GLIAL CELLS. Housekeeping and support cells of the neurons in the brain.

HISTOLOGY. The study of tissues that are groups of cells with a similar function.

HYPOTHALAMUS. A part of the forebrain that controls the pituitary gland and visceral functions such as water balance, body temperature, and sleep.

LIMBIC SYSTEM. That section of the brain concerned with emotional behavior.

MEDULLA OBLONGATA. A part of the hindbrain that controls most of the life functions.

MENINGES. A set of three membranes that protect the brain and spinal cord.

MICROTOME. A device that cuts thin sections of tissue for viewing under a microscope.

NEOCORTEX. The outer layer of the brain, which is the center of intellect and imagination, the "human" brain.

NEURON. A specialized cell of the nervous system that conducts an impulse.

NEUROLOGY. The study of the nervous system.

NEUROTRANSMITTER. A chemical messenger of the nervous system that can excite or inhibit the passage of a nerve impulse.

OLFACTORY LOBES. The parts of the brain that are responsible for the sense of smell.

OSCILLOSCOPE. A device that shows on a screen the current and voltage changes of electricity.

PARKINSON'S DISEASE. A disease of the brain characterized by muscle tremors and slow movements.

PEPTIDES. Small segments of proteins composed of amino acids.

PHRENOLOGY. A theory that a man's character and intelligence can be determined by the bumps on his skull.

PHYSIOLOGY. The study of the processes and activities of life.

PITUITARY. A gland at the base of the brain that secretes hormones that control other hormones.

RECEPTOR SITES. Areas on the membrane of a neuron where particular neurotransmitters fit as precisely as a lock and key.

SYNAPSE. A gap between the axon of one neuron and the dendrites of another neuron.

SYNAPTIC CLEFT. Another name for a synapse.

THALAMUS. A portion of the forebrain that acts as a main relay center for impulses going to the cerebrum.

TREPANNING. The ancient surgical technique of cutting a hole in a skull.

VENTRICLES. Spaces within the brain filled with cerebrospinal fluid.

Bibliography

Appelbaum, Stephen A. *Out in Inner Space: A Psychoanalyst Explores the New Therapies.* New York: Anchor Press/ Doubleday and Co., 1979.

Apsler, Alfred. *From Witch Doctor to Biofeedback: The Story of Healing by Suggestion.* New York: Julian Messner, 1977.

Asimov, Isaac. *Asimov's Biographical Encyclopedia of Science and Technology.* New York: Avon Books, 1976.

Bakan, Paul. "The Right Brain Is the Dreamer." *Psychology Today,* November, 1976, reprint No. P-370.

Barber, Theodore Xenophon. *LSD, Marihuana, Yoga, and Hypnosis.* Chicago: Aldine Publishing Company, 1970.

Blakemore, Colin. *Mechanics of the Mind.* Cambridge: Cambridge University Press, 1977.

Brown, Barbara. *New Mind, New Body: Biofeedback, New Directions for the Mind.* New York: Harper & Row Publishers, 1974.

Calder, Nigel. *The Mind of Man.* New York: The Viking Press, 1970.

Chase, Michael H. "The Matriculating Brain." *Psychology Today,* June 1973, reprint no. P-144.

Conway, Flo, and Siegelman, Jim. *Snapping.* New York: Dell Publishing Company, 1979.

Cowan, W. Maxwell. "The Development of the Brain." *Scientific American,* September, 1979, pp. 112–33.

Crick, F. H. C. "Thinking About the Brain." *Scientific American,* September 1979, pp. 219–32.

Delgado, José M. R. *Evolution of Physical Control of the Brain.* New York: The American Museum of Natural History, 1965.

Deutsch, J. Anthony. "Neural Basis of Memory." *Psychology Today,* May 1968, reprint no. P-24.

Dimond, E. Grey. *More Than Herbs and Acupuncture.* W. W. Norton & Co., 1975.

Edwards, Betty. *Drawing on the Right Side of the Brain.* Los Angeles: J. P. Tarcher, 1979.

Evarts, Edward V. "Brain Mechanisms of Movement." *Scientific American,* September 1979, pp. 164–79.

Ferguson, Marilyn. *The Brain Revolution: The Frontiers of Mind Research.* New York: Taplinger Publishing Co., 1973.

Freedman, Russell, and Morris, James E. *The Brains of Animals and Man.* New York: Holiday House, 1972.

Furst, Charles. *Origins of the Mind: Mid-Brain Connections.* Englewood Cliffs, N.J.: Prentice-Hall, 1979.

Goleman, Daniel. "A New Computer Test of the Brain." *Psychology Today,* May 1976, reprint no. P-336.

Geschwind, Norman. "Specializations of the Human Brain." *Scientific American,* September 1979, pp. 180–99.

Gilling, Dick. "The Keys of Paradise," transcript from *NOVA,* WGBH Educational Foundation, Boston, 1979.

Goldstein, Kenneth K. *New Frontiers of Medicine.* Boston: Little, Brown & Company, 1974.

"Guide For the Care and Use of Laboratory Animals." U.S. Department of Health, Education, and Welfare, NIH publication no. 80–23, 1980.

Halacy, Daniel S., Jr. *Bionics: The Science of "Living" Machines.* New York: Holiday House, 1965.

Halstead, Ward C., and Rucker, William B. "Memory: A Molecular Maze." *Psychology Today,* June 1968, reprint no. P-35.

Hart, Leslie A. *How the Brain Works.* New York: Basic Books, 1975.

Hubel, David H. "The Brain." *Scientific American,* September 1979, pp. 44–53.

Hyde, Margaret O. *Your Brain—Master Computer.* New York: McGraw-Hill Book Company, 1964.

Iversen, Leslie L. "The Chemistry of the Brain." *Scientific American,* September 1979, pp. 134–49.

Jones, Hardin, and Jones, Helen. *Sensual Drugs.* Cambridge: Cambridge University Press, 1977.

Kamiya, Joseph. "Conscious Control of Brain Waves." *Psychology Today,* April 1968, reprint no. P-49.

Kandel, Eric R. "Small Systems of Neurons." *Scientific American,* September 1979, pp. 66–76.

Keen, Sam. "A Conversation with John Lilly." *Psychology Today,* December 1971, reprint no. P-124.

Klemm, W. R. *Science, the Brain and our Future.* New York: Pegasus, 1972.

Landis, Dylan. "A Scan for Mental Illness." *Discover,* October 1980, pp. 26–28.

Lausch, Erwin. *Manipulation: Dangers and Benefits of Brain Research.* New York: The Viking Press, 1974.

Luce, Gay G., and Segal, Julius. *Sleep.* New York: Coward-McCann, 1966.

Mark, Vernon H. "A Psychosurgeon's Case for Psychosurgery." *Psychology Today,* July 1974, reprint no. P-185.

Melzack, Ronald. *The Puzzle of Pain.* New York: Basic Books, 1973.

Nauta, Walle J. H., and Feirtag, Michael. "The Organization of the Brain." *Scientific American,* September 1979, pp. 88–111.

Ornstein, Robert E. "Right and Left Thinking." *Psychology Today,* May 1973, reprint no. P-126.

Pines, Maya. *The Brain Changers.* New York: Harcourt Brace Jovanovich, 1973.

Ramón y Cajal, Santiago. *Recollections of My Life.* Philadelphia: The American Philosophical Society, 1937.

Restak, Richard. "The Brain Makes Its Own Narcotics." *Saturday Review,* March 5, 1977, pp. 7–11.

Reynolds, Vernon. *The Biology of Human Action.* San Francisco: W. H. Freeman and Co., 1976.

Russell, George K. *Marihuana Today.* New York: Myrin Institute for Adult Education, 1978.

Sagan, Carl. *The Dragons of Eden.* New York: Random House, 1977.

Snyder, Solomon. *Madness and the Brain.* New York: McGraw-Hill Book Co., 1974.

Sperber, Perry A. *Drugs, Demons, Doctors and Disease.* St. Louis, Mo.: Warren H. Green, 1973.

Stevens, Charles F. "The Neuron." *Scientific American,* September 1979, pp. 54–65.

Stevens, Leonard A. *Explorers of the Brain.* New York: Alfred A. Knopf, 1971.

———. *Neurons, Building Blocks of the Brain.* New York: Thomas Y. Crowell Co., 1974.

Taylor, Gordon Rattray. *The Natural History of the Mind.* New York: E. P. Dutton, 1979.

Ter-Pogossian, Michel M.; Raichle, Marcus E.; and Sobel, Burton E. "Positron-Emission Tomography." *Scientific American,* October 1980, pp. 171–81.

Thorwald, Jürgen. *Science and Secrets of Early Medicine.* Harcourt, Brace & World, 1962.

Villet, Barbara. "Opiates of the Mind." *Atlantic Monthly,* June 1978, pp. 82–89.

Weiss, Malcolm E. *The World Within the Brain.* New York: Julian Messner, 1974.

Wiley, James. *Beasts, Brains, & Behavior.* New York: The Four Winds Press, 1963.

Wittrock, M. C. *The Human Brain.* Englewood Cliffs, N.J.: Prentice-Hall, 1977.

Wyckoff, James. *Franz Anton Mesmer.* Englewood Cliffs, N.J.: Prentice-Hall, 1975.

Index

pain not felt by, 16, 34, 65
protection for, from outside forces, 16
redundancy in, 68
research on, 3, 4, 6, 7, 21, 24, 29, 50, 77, 101, 102, 103, 104–105
right, 72–78 *passim*, 103
sizes of, comparative, 14, 15
transplant of, 4, 105
tumor of, 46, 47, 104
ventricles of, 16, 20
weight of, 15
Brain Research Institute (UCLA), 41
Brain waves, 37, 38, 39, 41, 42, 43, 44, 54
Brainwashing, 96, 97–98, 99
Brindley, G. S., 92
Broca, Pierre Paul, 32, 33, 34
Broca's area, 33

Calder, Nigel, 66
California Institute of Technology, 42, 73
Cancer, 60, 89, 97, 102
CAT scan (computerized axial tomography), 47, 48, 49, 104
Caton, Richard, 37, 38
Cell membrane, 51, 56, 57
Cells, nerve. *See* Neurons (nerve cells)
Cerebellum, 10
Cerebrospinal fluid, 16
Cerebrum, 10, 11–12
hemispheres of, 15, 72–78, 103
See also Brain; Cortex, cerebral
Chlorpromazine, 56, 95
Clots, blood, 46
Cocaine, 95, 96
Computer, 6, 41, 42, 47, 91, 102
Conway, Flo, 98, 99
Corpus callosum, 73, 74, 76, 77
Cortex, cerebral, 12, 13, 15, 33, 34, 60, 71
See also Brain; Cerebrum
Crick, Francis, 6
Cult members, brainwashing of, 98–99
Cytoplasm of nerve cell, 15, 23

Dale, Henry, 53
Death, legal definition of, 39

Delgado, José, 90, 91
Delta waves, 38
Dendrites, 15, 23, 27, 51
Depression, 38, 54, 56, 84
PETT scanner for diagnosis of, 49
Diabetes, and biofeedback to regulate insulin levels, 46
Dickens, Charles, 80
Dinosaurs, 13
Discover, 49
DNA (deoxyribonucleic acid), 4, 6, 76
Dolphins, intelligence of, 13, 14
Dopamine, 54, 56
Drawing on the Right Side of Your Brain (Edwards), 75
Dreams, 79, 81, 82, 83
damming of, 82, 83
Drug addiction, 54, 55, 56, 57, 61
"Drug scene," 97
Du Bois-Reymond, Emil, 20, 21
Dura mater, 16
Dyslexia, 77, 103

Eccles, John, 7, 51
Edison, Thomas, 84
Edwards, Betty, 75
EEG (electroencephalogram), 37–44 *passim*, 46, 80, 81, 82, 103
Egypt, ancient, 5, 79
Einstein, Albert, 15, 77
Electricity
"animal," 18, 19, 20, 21, 51, 86
galvanic, 19
measurement of, 20
nerve, 21
Electrodes, use of, 34, 36, 37, 38, 42, 45, 78, 79, 90, 91, 92, 104
Elliotson, John, 87
Endorphin(s), 55, 61, 62
alpha, 61
beta, 60, 61, 62
gamma, 61
Engram, 63, 69
Enkephalin(s), 54, 59, 60, 61, 62
Epilepsy, 65, 87, 103
and biofeedback, 46
H.M. as patient with, 64, 65
W.J. as patient with, 73, 74, 75
Epinephrine, 56
"Errorless learning," 42

ESB (electrostimulation), 34, 36, 37
Extrasensory perception, 39, 46

Fender, Derek, 42
Fire-walking, 45
Forebrain, 10
Franklin, Benjamin, 87
Freud, Sigmund, 87, 95
Fritsch, Gustav, 34, 37
Frogs' legs, experiments on, 17–19,
    21, 50

Gage, Phineas, 29, 30, 31, 32, 34, 64,
    73, 92
Gajdusek, Daniel, 103
Galen (Claudius Galenus), 19, 20, 102
Gall, Franz Joseph, 33, 39
Galvani, Luigi, 17, 18, 19, 20, 50, 85,
    102
Galvanometer, 20, 21
Gazzaniga, Michael, 73
Genetic code, 4
Glial cells, 16
Goldstein, Avram, 56, 58, 60
Goleman, Daniel, 76
Golgi, Camillo, 24, 28, 102
Golgi's stain, 24, 26
Grana, Francesco, 104
Guillotin, Joseph, 87

Hallucinations, 82, 83, 96
Harlow, J. M., 30
Helmholtz, Hermann von, 21
Heroin, 55, 61, 95
Hess, Walter, 34, 36
Hindbrain, 10
Hippocampus, 10, 64, 65
Hippocrates, 73
Hitler, Adolf, 97, 103
Hitzig, Eduard, 34, 37
Hoffmann, Albert, 96
Hologram, 69, 70
Hooke, Robert, 22
Hughes, John, 59
Hypnosis, 56, 85, 87, 88, 89
    uses of, 89
Hypothalamus, 10, 11, 36

Impulse, nerve, 50–51, 52, 54
Intelligence, 13, 77
Interference pattern, produced by
    laser beams, 69

Interneurons, 16
IQ tests, 77

Jerry (chimpanzee), 41
Jet lag, 84
Jones, Jim, 98

Kamiya, Joseph, 44, 46
Kaufman, Joyce, 102
Kleitman, Nathaniel, 80
Kosterlitz, Hans, 59
Kuru, 103

Laser beams, 69, 104
Lashley, Karl, 65
Lavoisier, Antoine, 87
Learning, 15, 67, 68, 69, 70, 71, 99
    "errorless," 42
Leeman, Susan, 62
Left brain, 72–78 passim, 103
Levin, W., 92
Levy, Jerre, 102
Leyden jar, 17
Li, Choh Hao, 60, 61
Lilly, John, 13
Limbic system, 10, 11, 58, 60, 82
Lobotomy, 93–94
Loewi, Otto, 52, 53
LSD (lysergic acid diethylamide), 83,
    95, 96–97
L-tryptophan, 83

Marijuana, 95
McConnell, James, 66
McIntyre, Joan, 13
Meditation, 46
Medulla oblongata, 10
Memory, 63–71 passim
    ancestral (genetic), 63–64, 66, 81
    and H.M., case of, 64, 65
    holographic theory of, 69–70
    long-term, 63, 68
    short-term, 63, 64
    storage of, 66, 69, 70
Meninges, 16
Mesmer, Franz, 85–87, 88
Micropipette, 52
Microscope
    compound, 22
    electron, 51
Microtome, 23